The Best of BRITISH COMIC ART

Alan Clark

Boxtree

For all the comic artists who are not in this book but who will be in others . . .

Acknowledgements

All the illustrations in this book come from the author's own private collection, and are reproduced as historical illustrations to the text. Grateful acknowledgment is made to the publishers and the artists without whose contribution this book would not have been possible. The author is especially indebted to the following for permission to reproduce copyright material: Solo Syndication Ltd (for the *Daily Mail*); Collins Publishers; Fleetway Publications (Amalgamated Press, Odhams, and IPC material) and D. C. Thomson & Co. Ltd. All material originally published by D. C. Thomson & Co. Ltd. is reprinted by permission of D. C. Thomson & Co. Ltd. All material originally published by Fleetway Publications is reprinted by permission of Fleetway Publications.

Jacket illustrations © D. C. Thomson & Co. Ltd. and © Fleetway Publications, London, 1989.

Other books by Alan Clark

The Comic Art of Roy Wilson
The Comic Art of Reg Parlett
The Children's Annual: A History and Collector's Guide

The author is also the editor and publisher of *Golden Fun*; established in 1974, this was the world's first magazine devoted to British comics, story papers and annuals. Send SAE for details from: *Golden Fun*, 24 Arundel Road, Tunbridge Wells, Kent, TN1 1TB.

First published in Great Britain in 1989
by Boxtree Limited

© Alan Clark 1989

Designed by Groom and Pickerill
Typeset by Cambrian Typesetters, Frimley, Surrey
Printed and bound by Richard Clay Ltd, Bungay, Suffolk
For Boxtree Limited
36 Tavistock Street,
London WC2E 7PB

British Library Cataloguing in Publication Data
Clark, Alan, 1948–
Best of British comic art.
I. Title
741.5'942
ISBN 1-85283-264-9

Contents

Introduction

The history of comic art in Britain dates back to the 18th century, to the prints produced by William Hogarth, Thomas Rowlandson and James Gilray. These prints were single pictures, issued in both black and white and colour, and featured a complete range of subjects from the politically scurrilous to the raunchiest sexual encounters.

A boost was given to the art of comic illustration with the publication of *Punch* in 1841; after that, spin-offs abounded, two of the best being *Fun* (21 September 1861) and *Judy* (1 May 1867). From Hogarth on, the artists who drew the pictures, if not too modest to do so and when allowed by the publisher, put their names to their work. John Leech became the first *Punch* cartoonist to enjoy celebrity; he was followed by scores of others – cartoonists and illustrators who became household names.

James Henderson, the popular publisher of the Victorian era, issued *Funny Folks* – the first comic to appear in present-day format – on 12 December 1874. It was full of splendidly drawn pictures: some were political cartoons, others single picture jokes. Mention must also be made of *Ally Sloper's Half Holiday* (3 May 1884) published by Gilbert Dalziell. Ally Sloper had been introduced years earlier in *Judy*. His adventures were for the most part featured in single cartoons, the rest of the publication containing various jokes and drawings. This famous weekly helped to give comic art popular appeal. Henderson later followed *Funny Folks* with *Scraps* (29 August 1883) and *Snap-Shots* (28 July 1890). Both papers reprinted material from American magazines, mainly *Puck*, *Judge* and *Life*.

Another publisher who also used this material was Alfred Harmsworth (later Lord Northcliffe), whose first issues of *Comic Cuts* (17 May 1890) were comprised entirely of reprints. But Harmsworth was soon advertising for original material and offering 'handsome pay' for cartoons and funny drawings. *Comic Cuts* was a huge success (partly, it must be admitted, because it was half the price of the competition) and Harmsworth followed it immediately with a successor, *Illustrated Chips* (26 July 1890). There were also imitators in the form of *Funny Cuts* (2 July 1890) and others.

The contents of these comics generally were summed up in their titles: they contained 'scraps', 'chips', 'cuts' and other euphemisms for the single-picture joke. In due course, short sequences of related pictures began to appear, gradually becoming longer as the idea caught on. These were referred to as a 'set' of drawings, a term which stayed with the comics industry for the next 75 years and which is adopted in this book.

The most popular sets were those with regular characters. The first were a pair of tramps, Weary Willie and Tired Tim, who made their initial appearance on 16 May 1896 on page one of *Illustrated Chips*, drawn by one of the finest artists of the Victorian era, Tom Browne. Later that year the two tramps' adventures started to appear each week on the front page of *Chips*, and continued for an incredible 57 years. Browne drew them for only a short time; he was replaced by other artists, one of whom, Percy Cocking, drew Willie and Tim from 1909 until 1953. But whereas some people initially knew the identity of Tom Browne, few until recently were familiar with the name of the man who illustrated the set for the subsequent 44 years.

And there lies the rub. After the turn of the century, the weekly comics lowered their sights to the youth market as a newly educated populace found an extensive range of other material to absorb its interests. And as comics came to be aimed at children, artists' signatures were dropped and years of anonymity followed.

What could be called 'the dark ages of comic art' began around 1904 when Harmsworth's new weekly comic, *Puck*, was published, initially aimed at adults. Soon, however, a 'Puck Junior' was introduced, appealing directly to young children. Other publishers followed suit, and since that time comics have been synonymous with the children's market.

Because comics were for kids, could there be any reason why adults should ever look at them again, save to cast an eye over their children's reading matter to ensure it was acceptable? Indeed there was – and still is. Although plot lines might be thin, jokes weak and stories simple, the fact remains that within their pages is the work of some of the finest graphic artists Britain has ever produced. And the real injustice is that although most people are familiar with their drawings and characters, few can put a name to the illustrators who have given generations enormous pleasure. The work of some of these artists is the subject of this book.

Who are these unsung heroes? Well, let's start with the characters they drew. The comic adventures of Charlie Chaplin, for example, appeared in *The Funny Wonder* from August 1915 to June 1944. His artist was Albert 'Bertie' Thacker Brown whose career began in 1908 and lasted for 50 years – during which time he notched up an estimated half-million drawings. And he accomplished this astonishing feat without ever once adding a signature to his pictures.

Those other stars of the cinema, Laurel and Hardy, appeared in the famous weekly *Film Fun* for nearly three decades. They, together with their contemporaries Joe E. Brown, George Formby and others, were drawn by George William (Bill) Wakefield, whose career in comics lasted 35 years. Quick to emulate his father was son Terry, who began drawing for the comics in 1927 and contributed countless pages in his own 30-year career.

Most people have heard of Keyhole Kate and Hungry Horace, those psychotic stars of *The Dandy*, but only a select few know that the owner of the cryptic initials 'A. M.', which sometimes appeared in the bottom right-hand corner of the last panel, were those of Allan Morley, a comic artist of 40 years standing.

Admittedly, of all the hundreds of artists who did not sign their work, there were a tiny number who did. Yet even they have remained largely unrecognised. Two included in this book are Herbert Foxwell and Dudley Watkins. Their art was of the highest order and is an integral part of British comics' history. Foxwell was responsible for Tiger Tim and Teddy Tail; Watkins drew Desperate Dan and Lord Snooty.

The sixth and final artist whose work is represented here is Ken Reid. Reid's style was unique, each week delighting innumerable readers of the Provincial Press with 'The Adventures of Fudge the Elf'. After that he entertained as many more with 'Roger the Dodger' and 'Jonah' in the pages of *The Beano*; and, later still, with his funny-ugly creations 'Frankie Stein' and 'Faceache'.

This book features the best of British comic art; but of course it's not as simple as that, for there are scores of artists whose work merits this description. However, in order to provide a thorough and representative selection of illustrations, the list necessarily had to be pared down to six. Future books will perhaps include other artists, equally deserving of recognition and appreciation.

'BERTIE' BROWN

After a visit to the cinema in 1915, Bertie Brown suggested to his employers that the new screen comedian he had just seen would be ideal for comics adaptation. They agreed and the result is shown here on the front page of *The Funny Wonder*, 7 August 1915, Charlie Chaplin's first appearance anywhere in comic form. Brown was to draw Chaplin for nearly 30 years; no one ever did it better, his pen perfectly capturing the star's likeness. © Fleetway Publications, London, 1989.

Albert 'Bertie' Thacker Brown was the most prolific of all British comic artists. From 1908 until his retirement in 1959 he drew an estimated half a million or so pictures for thousands of sets (the term then given to comic strips) in scores of comics. There was scarcely an Amalgamated Press (AP) 'funnies' comic in which his work did not appear and almost everyone in the country over the age of 40 must have seen his work at one time or another. His brief, sketchy style was instantly recognisable with a freedom of line that was easy on the eye and made comics fun to read, but his name would have been unknown to his many readers since his drawings, according to the convention of the time, appeared anonymously.

'Bertie' Brown (another nickname, inevitably, was 'Buster') was born in 1887 in Epsom, Surrey. When he left school, he won a scholarship to the Slade School of Art, but was unable to accept due to his family's financial needs. Instead, he took a job with a business in Lewisham. A fan of the great Victorian artist Tom Browne, he visited him and was encouraged to try submitting one-off joke cartoons to the comic papers of the AP and James Henderson.

Henderson published a weekly named *Scraps* and it was there that Brown's work first appeared. A later submission to *Illustrated Chips*, an AP paper, brought him an offer of a staff job, working for Langton Townley, who had a keen eye and a genuine appreciation of comic art. Not every artist got this chance, the majority being freelance, working from home; clearly Townley had seen something special in the young man.

Brown began work for the AP by taking on various sets which had been started by experienced artists; it must have pleased him considerably when one of those artists turned out to be his idol, Tom Browne. But soon he began to submit his own sets, the first being 'Homeless Hector' (*Chips*: 1909), a peculiarly drawn dog with an endearing personality. It was popular enough to last for the remainder of *Chips*'s run; Hector was still appearing in the last issue of the pink weekly, published on 12 September 1953, three short of its 3,000th number.

Other sets of his own creation followed: 'Coffdrop College' (*Merry & Bright*: 1911); 'John Willie's Jackdaw' (*Comic Cuts*: 1911); 'Herr Kutz' (*The Butterfly*: 1913); 'Sally Cinders' (*The Favorite Comic*: 1915) and 'Cyril Slapdab' (*Merry & Bright*: 1913). In a few short years he had proved himself one of the most versatile artists in the AP's employ.

He was fortunate in the First World War: called up in his late twenties, in 1916, he joined the Royal Field Artillery but spent the war based at Woolwich Barracks in the drawing

CHARLIE CHAPLIN APPEARS TO-DAY. CHARLIE CHAPLIN

VOL. II.—No. 72.] EVERY TUESDAY. [WEEK ENDING AUGUST 7, 1915.

CHARLIE CHAPLIN, the Scream of the Earth (*the famous Essanay Comedian*).

1. Here he is, readers! Good old Charlie! Absolutely IT! A scream from start to finish. What's he doing now, eh? "'Twas here," says he, standing in a graceful posish. by an artistically designed coal-hole, with the faithful hound attached to his cane: "'Twas here I was to meet Maggie! Phwpsts!" But see! A rival approaches!

2. Then the rival, one Esmond MacSydeslyppe Hugo Balscadden O'Chuckitupp—the rival, we repeat, did a bit of dirty work. Fact! He held forth a tempting bone, and Charlie's faithful hound cast the eye of approval on same. Base rival! "Soon," says the chirpy Charlie, putting on another fag: "Soon she will be here. Oh, joy!"

3. But the hound, deciding to do the chew on the bone, legged it up the paving stones, taking Charlie's stick with him. And Charlie, with his visible means of support thus removed, did a graceful flop into said coal-hole just as the lovely Maggie appeared! "Charlie!" said she, with much spurnery, "What do you think you're doing?"

4. Ha! Enter the rival! "Don't you have anything to do with him, Maggie," says the rival: "He's absolutely sale price, he is. Marked down to one-and-nine-three—him! Come with me to some nook, where we may hold converse!"

5. So off they went to the nook, but Charlie was soon up and doing. Yea! He flopped along, soon coming upon the rival telling the tale of love to the beauteous one. "Ho!" says he. "Now to get a portion of my own back! Now for it!"

6. Well, the rival was just on the point of laying his riches at the damsel's dainty patent number two's, when Charlie, picking up a dustbin (full flavour) which happened to be handy, shoved it into his outstretched fins. Which did it—yes!

7. Up jumped the young person. Talk about the frozen eye! Wow! "Sir-r!" she said: "I did not come here to be entertained by such poltroonery. Please remove yourself forthwith. Your face causes me uneasiness! No explanations, please! Get hence and proceed to climb trees for mushrooms. All is over between us!" Or words to that effect. Then Charlie did the inward chuckle, and raised his hat with courtly grace.

8. And he did the affable and endearing chat that completely restored him to favour in the damsel's eyes. "Permit me to suggest," says this gallant old filbert, "a light lunch at the Café de Chancitt, with a jaunt on the merry old motor-'bus to follow. Having just received my quarterly allowance—not half—all is well. Let us proceed!" And they did proceed—some! More news next week, so look out!

A MERRY CHRISTMAS TO ALL OUR READERS.

VOL. II.—No. 92.] EVERY TUESDAY. [WEEK ENDING DECEMBER 25, 1915.

CHARLIE CHAPLIN, The Scream of the Earth (*The Famous Essanay Comedian*).

1. Dear Old Tops and Nuts,—'Twas somewhat snowy, and all that sort of silly nonsense, but I took my ease against a street corner, and did the doze. Some slumber, my bonny boys. What-ho! The dream! Wh-z-z-z! Ay, ay!

2. But some merry nippers had made a slide in front of me, the noo! Well, the jolly old snow kept doing the drop, and it seems that I looked like a bit of a snowman after a while. So up pops a cop—

3. In a frantically joyous mood, and he says: "What-ho, man, are you a snowman?" And he gives me a shove with his baton. Then he goes and does the tap on the window. So I said: "O! Some points to be watched here!"

4. Bless your old bootlaces, I wasn't slow! Not it! With the deft shove, I popped cane under his hearty helmet, and applied the trotter to the back of his overcoat. "Ha!" says he. "Ho for the chewable Christmas pudding! Sugar and spice, and all that's nice!" says he, dear old chaps. Then the aroma of the pud made itself felt.

5. Mphsms! Myumyum! That was a pudding and a half, if you like, dear students. So, as Cora, the cook, raised the window, I hoiked off the hero's helmet, and bunged him a touch with the trotter that sent him skidding along that slide at, I estimate, 90 miles per hour. Do I miss much? Nay, nay, Pauline! Not a bit of it. I don't think so!

6. Then I adopted his helmet (looking well in it, too, if I tell you), and extended the fin, in professional fashion, cookwards. And lo! I captured the pudding, old villagers. Some capture, too, believe me, the noblest Roman of them all. And there was jolly old Bob licking along on the slide, well into the background. Ho, ho! Well, as I say, I snaffled that pudding—

7. And away I went with some celerity. See footmarks. D'ye like Christmas pudding, boys? D'ye appreciate the flavour? Whoho! I've wrapped myself round some puddings in my career, old chickens; but this one was the absolute last word in cookery. My word, that damsel could do the roast and boiled! Whpts!—Your one and only, CHARLIE CHAPLIN

office, where he was sometimes called upon to paint scenery for target practice. He was also a driver for a time and became well known for his ability to draw likenesses of his fellow soldiers.

Throughout his time in the army, he still produced work for the comics, and one character in particular. In the summer of 1915, he visited the cinema to see a new comedy star who had the audience in stitches. The star was Essanay Studio's Charlie Chaplin, who Brown immediately realised was perfect for comic strip adaptation. At Brown's suggestion, the editor of *The Funny Wonder* immediately sought permission from Essanay Studio, who readily agreed, obviously appreciating the publicity to be gained. The first Chaplin set appeared on the front page of the issue dated 7 August 1915, brilliantly depicted by Bertie Brown. It was the first of more than a thousand he was to draw over the next 30 or so years. No one ever drew Chaplin better.

After the armistice, Bertie Brown returned to his position on the staff of the AP, which in 1912 had moved to Fleetway House in Farringdon Street,

London, EC4. His output was enormous, drawing around six or seven pages a week, but despite his busy schedule he was always willing to help new artists, both with drawing tips and ideas for scripts (which artists had to write themselves in those days). Reg Parlett, an 85-year-old veteran of the comics business – and still drawing! – is Britain's greatest living comic artist. (He is the subject of a separate work: *The Comic Art of Reg Parlett*: Golden Fun Publishing, 1986.) Parlett met Brown when he joined the AP and remembers him thus: 'Bertie Brown was one of the best and most prolific of the artists working for the Amalgamated Press when I joined in the early Twenties. I knew him well as we lived close to one another and became good friends. Bertie was only too glad to give me, or any artist, the benefit of his experience by giving useful criticism and advice whenever he was

Above
Chaplin appeared on page one of *The Funny Wonder* until 1932 and then moved inside – still drawn by Bertie Brown – until the early Forties. Starting with no more than eight pictures, the number of panels was increased to around a dozen (see opposite) and then cut back to eight as Chaplin's screen popularity declined. At first, Brown's Chaplin was a careful rendering of his celluloid image; later, he allowed himself more freedom, with a looser style which obviously suited him better.
© Fleetway Publications, London, 1989.

Opposite
A few months later Brown illustrated this wonderful, rare Christmas Number of 75 years ago.
© Fleetway Publications, London, 1989.

Brown drew many front pages for *Sparkler*. One such was 'The Flighty Pranks of Freddie Flip and Uncle Bunkle' (20 April 1935); shown here are reproductions of some of the original drawings. This was moved to an inside page after a few issues and assigned to Bill Wakefield. It is interesting to compare Brown's drawings on this page with those by Wakefield elsewhere in this book. © Fleetway Publications, London, 1989.

called upon to do so. He was highly respected by all who knew him and his work.'

Bertie Brown drew for an extraordinarily extensive range of comics. He seemed equally at home with the nursery comics (*Bubbles*, *Rainbow*), the upmarket weeklies which parents bought for their children (*Puck*) and the popular comics printed in black ink on white or coloured paper, which, at a penny, cost half the price of the others. His brilliant art was enjoyed by all types of readership. Brown never skimped on the backgrounds of his pictures. He always included characters who were a part of everyday life: tradesmen, shopkeepers, policemen, soldiers, types of all sorts and, very often, pretty young women. He was particularly good at drawing the last, undoubtedly inspired by his beautiful young wife, Maisie.

During the 1920s Brown created several picture sets which lasted for years, each a classic of the genre. One of these was 'Moonlight Moggie', the feline equivalent of his earlier 'Homeless Hector', which was still running in *Chips*. Moggie was a black cat whose adventures began in *The Jolly Jester* in 1920 and lasted 33 years until the last issue of *Chips*, where she shared a final appearance with Hector (drawn by Brown).

Brown showed true genius, however, when he was put to work in 1926 to create a new front page set for the *Butterfly*. The result was 'Smiler and Smudge' (the chums of Carraway College), a tall white boy and his small black chum. Years ahead of its time, 'Smiler & Smudge' did for racial harmony then what society has only recently been trying to get to grips with: showing black and white on equal terms. Sixty years ago it would have been easy to fall into the trap of making Smudge the butt of the jokes and to use cliché as humour. But Brown never allowed this to happen. Actually it was Smiler who frequently ended up as both loser and victim in their adventures and rivalries, outmanoeuvred and outclassed by his smart black chum. Brown drew the feature beautifully. His characters were always fluid, never stiff, and genuinely funny.

Bertie Brown's other memorable features between the two World Wars were comedy teams. One was 'Big Ben and Little Len' (1927), two brothers who lived with their long-suffering father; it was an agreeable, if fairly ordinary, small set produced for the centre pages of *Comic Cuts*. But the others, though similar, were considerably more original. 'Pa Perkins and his Son Percy' first appeared in *Chips* in 1922; its worthy successor, and easily the better of the two, was 'Dad Walker and his Son Wally' which began on the front page of the first issue of *Larks*, 29 October 1927.

Constable Cuddlecook had begun his comic capers as long ago as 1909, drawn by G. M. Payne, who was also a renowned postcard artist. Bertie Brown drew the character for the front page of *Jester* for most of the Twenties and Thirties. © Fleetway Publications, London, 1989.

One set that Bertie Brown took over from another artist and made his own was 'Constable Cuddlecook', which he drew during the 1920s and 1930s. 'Cuddy' was a comical copper who wore a helmet several times too small, and spent his time chasing crafty crooks and saucy scoundrels. For years he was 'Britain's favourite Bluebottle', appearing on the front page of *The Jester*.

Brown had shown his gift for capturing a likeness with 'Charlie Chaplin'. It seems odd, then, that of all the comic titles he drew for during the 1920s and 1930s, the famous AP weekly *Film Fun* was not among them. But perhaps not so strange if it

Reproduction of some original artwork for 'Constable Cuddlecook', featuring a typical 'wheeze'.

© Fleetway Publications, London, 1989.

Opposite
Here's wishing a jolly Jubilee Day to you and all jolly Jesterites,' says Constable Cuddlecook in this rare Jubilee Number, dated 11 May 1935. The celebration was for George V.
© Fleetway Publications, London, 1989.

No. 1,748.

THE COMICAL CAPERS OF CONSTABLE CUDDLECOOK.

MAY 11TH, 1935.

1. Dear Mr. Editor, My Posh Old Playmate,—I thought I'd better look extra-smart for the jolly old Jubilee, so I got out the ironing-board and started to crease my trousers.

2. So engrossed was I in my task, I failed to observe that Cute Clarence, one of my prison pets, had hooked the cell key with one of those jolly paper squeakers you blow out.

3. And while I held my trousers up to admire, Clarence unlocked the door of his cell and crept out on all fours. "'S'easy!" that saucy scoundrel was saying, as he departed.

4. But I soon made things warm for him, sir! Mps! As he crept past, he didn't see the iron in my hand. I'm afraid he got rather scorched in the region of the hip-pocket!

5. After that, Cute Clarence showed a burning desire for some fresh air, and before I could stop him he was leaping through the open window. "Too hot here!" he piped.

6. "Help! Prisoner escaped!" I yelled, dashing off in pursuit, and nearly bursting my lungs blowing my whistle. Seeing me coming, Clarence darted up the town hall steps.

7. What a surprise I got when I ran right into the jolly old Mayor of Mudville, who was just coming down the steps. Of course, it was really Clarence dressed in the mayor's togs, but I wasn't to know that at the time, was I, sir? Fancy!

8. His washup—I mean, his worship—told me I'd got to be his train-bearer, then! I started to tell him all about the prisoner I was trying to catch, but he wouldn't listen. "No argufying!" he cried. "Do as your mayor tells you—see?"

9. We were walking along peaceably, when four legs and some fur came tearing round the corner. 'Twas a cat named Minnie the Moocher, and a dog was chasing it for having stolen its dinner! Minnie took refuge in the mayor's train!

10. The dog followed the cat, and a cat-and-dog fight followed that! Climbing a post out of the danger-zone, I watched points, and my peepers nearly popped out when the mayor's train fell off, revealing Cute Clarence underneath!

11. With my prisoner caught, collared, and captured, I toddled with him back to the town hall, where the real mayor was nearly off his rocker because he couldn't find his robes! "You must stay to the banquet, Cuddy!" he cooed. Aha!

12. And that's how I got a seat of honour next to his Honour at the Jubilee banquet! I enjoyed the finest feast I've had since the last one! Here's wishing a jolly Jubilee Day to you and all jolly Jesterites!—CONSTABLE CUDDLECOOK.

Brown drew this lively set for the centre pages of *Illustrated Chips* for 31 years (1922–53). All three characters are excellent but Pa Perkins is particularly well-observed. This example is from *Chips* Christmas Number, 28 December 1929. © Fleetway Publications, London, 1989.

is remembered that the editor of *Film Fun* was Fred Cordwell, a devotee of Bill Wakefield (see p. 39), who instructed his artists to restrict themselves to his style. Brown's freedom of line and sketchy approach would no doubt have been anathema to Cordwell; and for Brown to have been forced to adhere to the rigid accuracy of Cordwell's demands would have been equivalent to donning a straight-jacket. It was only after Cordwell died, in 1948, that the new editor, Phil Davis, dared to introduce Bertie Brown's penmanship to the pages of *Film Fun*.

Nevertheless there were other outlets for his skill in drawing personalities: the editor of *The Jolly Comic* asked him to draw Will Hay for the front page in 1936. This was broadly derived from Hay's highly successful films in which he played an incompetent schoolmaster. It ran for about three years. *Radio Fun*, a new weekly launched in 1938, also provided scope for his talents. Beginning with the now almost-forgotten Richard Hassett (1940), he went on to depict many of the popular stars of Forties' wireless, including Vic Oliver, Sally Rogers, Charlie Chester,

Opposite
As the editor said: 'You want the best laughs? Here they are!' All provided, of course, by Bertie Brown and Smiler and Smudge, the front page stars of *Butterfly*. And what a beautiful title-block illustration he drew for this Easter Number from the Golden Age of comics! © Fleetway Publications, London, 1989.

BUTTERFLY. EVERY TUESDAY

YOU WANT THE BEST LAUGHS? HERE THEY ARE!

No. 941. EIGHT PAGES OF FUN AND STORY. APRIL 20, 1935.

THE ADVENTURES OF SMILER AND SMUDGE, THE BUTTERFLY BOYS.

1. One Bun-day morning, Smiler and Smudge set out from Carraway College in the direction of the river. Both were armed with fishing tackle, but the coon was one-armed with buns, which he was carrying in a very large-sized bag.

2. Doctor Cake was to award a prize for the best fish caught, you see, but it certainly didn't look as if Smiler were going to get it when he drew up out of the river the teeniest of tiddlers you could think of.

3. " 'Tcha ! " chirped Smudge. " How can you'se expect any self-respectin' fish to come after dose mouldy breadcrumbs dat you'se using for bait ? Why not gib dem some nice tasty hot cross buns ? "

4. And so chirping, he strung a couple to his own line and dropped them into the water. " Dey'll make de old fish faces brighten up ! " breezed the coon. " Why, I do believe I'se caught something already ! " And the boat began to rock to and fro.

5. " Phew ! " panted the coon, as he struggled to pull his line in. " I didn't know dat any whales grew in dis ribber, but I feels as if dat's what's entangled on de end ob my line ! " And then with a long pull and strong pull, both at once, he managed a to get that aquatic creature out of its bed in the river. The coon was surprised when he saw it, too !

6. So was Smiler ! " Coo ! " he cried. " You laughed at what I caught, Smudgie, but I'd sooner have my catch than yours ! There's not room for all of us in this boat now ! " And to make room for the fish, the obliging laddie leapt overboard, leaving the coon alone.

7. That is to say, he left the coon alone with the fish, but that didn't seem to suit the resident of the river. It wanted to be alone on its own, and it wasn't very long in showing Smudge the way out of the boat. And it finished this up by giving the coon a very smart slap with its fin !

8. Then, being a wise old fish, it made itself comfy in the boat and took charge of the big bag of buns. Meanwhile, Smiler and Smudge were making the acquaintance of each other beneath the water. " Glug ! " gurgled Smiler. " Got any ideas, coon ? " " Glug ! " gurgled Smudge. " Yes ! "

9. And then he gurgled to his chum his idea to push the boat along towards the shore. This they did, giving the fish a joy-ride all the way. It wasn't the only thing the fish was having either, for it was golloping up the buns at a fast and furious rate. " Nearly dere now, Smiler ! " called Smudge.

10. But when they landed on the shore, they didn't stop there, but pushed the boat with its fishy passenger all the way to the college. " How's this for a catch, sir ? " they shouted. " Well, well, well ! " wuffed the old doc. " That's a splendiferous sample of fishery ! " And he presented the prize. Oh, what a bun !

The flags were flying on the front page of *Butterfly* on 15 May 1937 for this magnificent Coronation issue. National celebrations always brought out the best in comic artists. Here, Bertie Brown superbly takes Smiler and Smudge to George VI's Coronation.
© Fleetway Publications, London, 1989.

Left
During the Thirties, British comics' most celebrated one-parent family was Dad Walker and his son, Wally. Their adventures were chronicled by Brown in more than 7,500 pictures in 656 issues of *Larks* during a continuous run of 13 years. This jolly New Year page (*opposite*) is part of a continuing saga about 'The Old Crocks' Race', a race with old cars which they eventually won with their entry 'Thunderbolt'.
© Fleetway Publications, London, 1989.

No. 585. **DAD WALKER AND WALLY HAVE SOME NEW YEAR LARKS IN THE "OLD CROCKS' RACE."** JANUARY 7, 1939.

1. Dear LARKS Lovers,—We were chugging along through the snow and night in the Old Crocks' Race when I suddenly remembered it was New Year's Eve and decided to celebrate.

2. Having donged the old year well and truly out, we got on our way. I thought I heard the sirens doing their stuff, but we discovered it was Thunderbolt's back axle squeaking.

3. "Rattling radiators!" I gasped, as I felt old Thunderbolt's pulse and peeped in the back axle box. "There's not enough juice in here to draw a tadpole. Get a can out, Wally."

4. Well, we proceeded to give the cogs a drink of grease, and up buzzed our rivals, Black Jack and Red Herrin, a proper pair of trouble-makers, all ripe for a spot of bother.

5. "What-ho, Walker!" warbled Black Jack, giving me his hoof instead of his hand. "We'll hide the chopper—I mean, bury the hatchet and start the New Year well, eh?"

6. I went sprawling with one flipper in the grease, and old Black Jack pushed out his mitt. "Walker-boy," he chirped, "We've done some murky work, but now we'll be clean."

7. That suited me, old pals, but we didn't start the New Year clean after all, for old Black Jack got a handful of axle grease, and Red Herrin got an eyeful all to himself. Ha, ha!

8. Of course, I said I was sorry and all that, but Black Jack just wouldn't hark. He prepared to knock me up a catcher, but only managed to hand Red Herrin a good thump.

9. "Phew! This is no place for us, Wal," I gasped "Let's go!" I made a bee-line for old Thunderbolt, and Black Jack galloped up vowing vengeance. But he slipped up

10. Yes, Red suddenly keeled over and kicked his pal into the pool of grease. "Ha, ha! There's many a slip." I chortled. "And here's where we slip off. Get going, Walter."

11. Things didn't stop there, though. Red Herrin skidded in the snow, biffed Black Jack and made him do a slide on his chin. "Ha, ha! Ta muchly for the push off!" I cooed.

12. They started to chase us, but we gave them another helping of grease and left them skating about like a brace of flies on a bald head.—Yours till mice moo, DAD WALKER.

(Don't miss the miles of smiles with Dad Walker and Wally in the "Old Crocks' Race" in LARKS on sale next Saturday.)

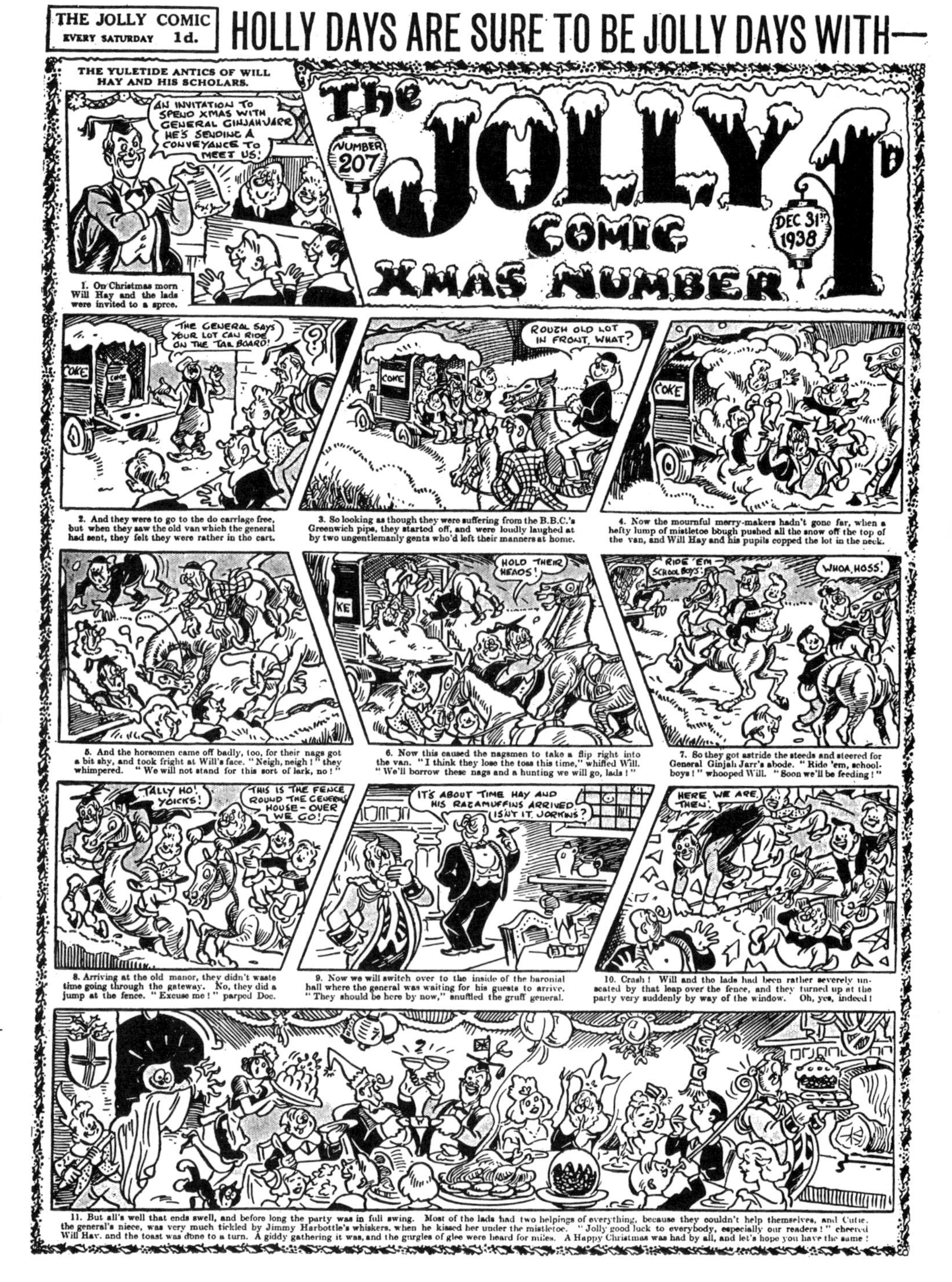

Right
Will Hay and his boys from St Michael's in festive mood in the Christmas Number of *The Jolly Comic*, 31 December 1938.
© Fleetway Publications, London, 1989.

Opposite
Years before Jack Warner said 'Evening All' to the millions who watched him on television in the Fifties in 'Dixon of Dock Green', he was a popular star of the stage and wireless. During the Forties he was drafted into the army for his appearances in *Radio Fun*, where he had to tangle not only with Hitler but also Sergeant Sossidgeskin and Colonel Cornplaster.
© Fleetway Publications, London, 1989.

Jack Warner and Derek Roy. There were also the superstars: Tommy Handley (who, it was said, was so fond of his appearances that he was never without a copy of *Radio Fun* in his pocket), Gracie Fields and the 'Take It From Here' team of Dick Bentley, Joy Nicholls and Jimmy Edwards. As a rule, photographs were used for reference but in the case of 'Take It From Here', Brown visited the studio to watch them in action and made sketches.

After the death of Fred Cordwell, Brown both initiated and took over from other artists popular movie stars' adventures appearing in *Film Fun*: Sid Field (1950), (Dean) Martin and (Jerry) Lewis (1954), Frankie Howerd (1956) and Harry Secombe (1957). Others included Frank Randle, Red Skelton and Cardew (The Cad) Robinson.

In the 1950s Brown found himself drawing for a new comic, a product of the television age: *TV Fun*, edited

1. A HAPPY CHRISTMAS, One and All !—Now let me tell you something ! Me Littel Gel and I were a-decorating the old barrack-room late on Christmas Eve, and it was no easy job trying to make the place look pretty with Sergeant Sossidgeskin buzzing around. It was not only his face that spoiled the effects, but his temper, too ! He groused about everything and said he couldn't see the point of Christmas decorations, but at that moment he tripped over a paper-chain, and started rubbing noses with some prickly holly. " Oh, golly ! " I chortled. " Isn't the holly jolly, Sarge ? "

2. The old non-com. pulled his Army socks up, and stamped off. He said he was going to bed, and would forget all about Christmas by dreaming of a plateful of stewed ills. Colonel Cornplaster was ril sorry Sargy wanted to forget about the festive season, so he dressed up like Santa Claus, and made himself a white, woolly, chin-drapery. " Are you going to go down Sarge's chimney ? " I asked. " No—I'm not on an offensive sweep," he said.

3. With his big boots on, Cornplaster tip-toed into Sargy's boudoir. He was as quiet as can be—well, he was so quiet that the boys two miles away could only just hear him. " Oh, put a sock in it ! " snarled Sarge, half asleep, but the C.O. put a present in the three-striper's sock. But he didn't oughter have done it ! You see, while we were making-up the Colonel, I knocked a lump of coal in his sack, and now that coal was in the sock.

4. Sargy was rill ratty about it. COSH ! He threw the lump of coal out of his door as if he was at the fair trying to knock a coconut off a stick. " My hat ! " I cried, when I saw where it was going to. " No ! My head ! " groaned Cornplaster. The Colonel turned round and caught Sarge twiddling his big toes on the doorstep. " YOU ! " he shrieked. " No, it's me," corrected Sossidgeskin. " That's enough ! " said Cornplaster. " Go to clink for hitting your superior officer on the crumpet while wearing only your pyjamas ! "

Jack Warner

REVNELL AND WEST - The Long & Short of it!

Bertie Brown drew many personalities for *Radio Fun*. 'The Long and the Short of It', Ethel Revnell and Gracie West, (*above*) were featured from the first issue in 1938 drawn by Reg Parlett; Brown took them over in the mid-Forties. Vic Oliver, 'The Whimsical Wisecracker', (*below*) had appeared on radio, the stage and in films when Bertie Brown began to draw him in 1941.
© Fleetway Publications, London, 1989.

by Stanley Gooch, who was also responsible for *Radio Fun*. Two pages featured women: Shirley Eaton and Diana Decker. (The two stars later appeared in various films; Eaton became world famous when she won the part of the 'golden girl' in the James Bond film *Goldfinger*.) For *Radio Fun* Brown drew that wonderful 1950s trio, the Beverley Sisters.

Bertie Brown's last published drawings appeared in 1959 when he was 72. But he continued working for the comics, scriptwriting (or 'wheeze-whacking', as he called it) for other artists for some years afterwards. He died in 1974. To vintage comics enthusiasts, Bertie Brown was one of the greats. He was – and still is – revered by fellow professionals and aficionados alike, and with good reason: for more than half a century he turned out hundreds of thousands of comic drawings which gave pleasure to millions. It is a sad irony that because of the traditional insistence on anonymity the public at large never knew his name.

The Coronation of Queen Elizabeth II in 1953 gave the comics good cause to celebrate. Here's Cardew 'The Cad' Robinson putting out the flags for the great day, celebrated within the pages of *Radio Fun*. © Fleetway Publications, London, 1989.

'The Editor Has Important News For You Inside' almost always heralds sad news for comics aficionados. The sad news in this case was the end of *Chips*, the weekly that began 63 years previously in 1890. Pictured here are the last 'Pa Perkins and Percy' and the final 'Homeless Hector and Moonlight Moggie'. Hector's last words are suitable for the occasion.
© Fleetway Publications, London, 1989.

Below
As could be expected, there was much of 'The Goon Show' in Harry Secombe's adventures in *Film Fun*. They were often totally outlandish but frequently hilarious. Here's Secombe in a typical wacky situation, as a bullfighter with a featherduster. This is one of Brown's final sets, published in May 1959; by this time it was the publisher's policy for all lettering within the speech balloons to be done 'in house'. Thus, Bertie Brown's delightfully characteristic lettering has disappeared.
© Fleetway Publications, London, 1989.

Opposite
Comic Life was bought by the Amalgamated Press in 1920. Bertie Brown started 'The Merry Boys of Dingle School' in 1923. This superb front page is from the Christmas Number of the following year.
© Fleetway Publications, London, 1989.

Puck had originally been published for adults but lowered its sights to the nursery market. However, it recovered some of its former sophistication for this delightful Christmas Number dated Christmas Day, 1915, with a front page by Bertie Brown.
© Fleetway Publications, London, 1989.

COMIC LIFE 2D. Xmas-Number.
GRAND XMAS TALES AND FUN FOR EVERYONE
Comic Life 2D.
GRAND XMAS No.
No. 1384
DEC. 27th 1924
CHARGE!
HA! HA! THAT'S ONE SNOW-MAN THE LESS!
THE merry mixed pupils of Dingle School built a jolly old snow man on Christmas morning, and they had just popped indoors to have some baked sarsaparillas and a glass of hot chestnuts when Percival the Porter appeared. "Pah! I'll soon have that down," he snorted and he charged it.
2. And that was how the poor old snow man met his downfall. But whilst this porter person was chuckling cheerily at his cleverness the artful Dingle-ites had hauled their toboggan up on to the roof. "Wha-ay—this is as good as being on the Alps," cried Billy Britain, as the toboggan toboggeđ down the roof.
OH WELL! BOYS WILL BE BOYS!
3. But it pushed a whole heap of snow down in front of it which shot over the edge of the roof and plumped down well and truly upon the porter. And that cold stuff filled up his ears and trickled down his back and made him feel glad that Christmas comes but once a year. He couldn't even move an eyelash.
4. "Tee-hee—Percival makee velly fine snow man," purred Ching Wun Fo. "Velly handsome one, too." "Thank you so much, dear Mr. Porter, for replacing our snow man," cooed Billy. "So kind of you." Fortunately, the snow cooled the wrath of the old fellow. "Oh well—boys will be boys," he said.
GO!
CRACK!
5. Then Dr. Dingle, with a sort of peace-and-good-will-to-all-men beam on his face, came bustling on to the scene. "Come along, boys," he cried. "The turkey awaits, and the pudding is yearning to be set alight. Percival, old fellow," said he, "you must join the merry party and forget all the pranks that these young rascals have played upon you since last Christmas, and all will be well." And all was well. After the dinner, during what time Dutchy distinguished himself as the greatest young trencherman since Friar Tuck, they played games, and the dear old doc. indulged in a little horseplay, while Percival did not seem to mind being made a donkey of.

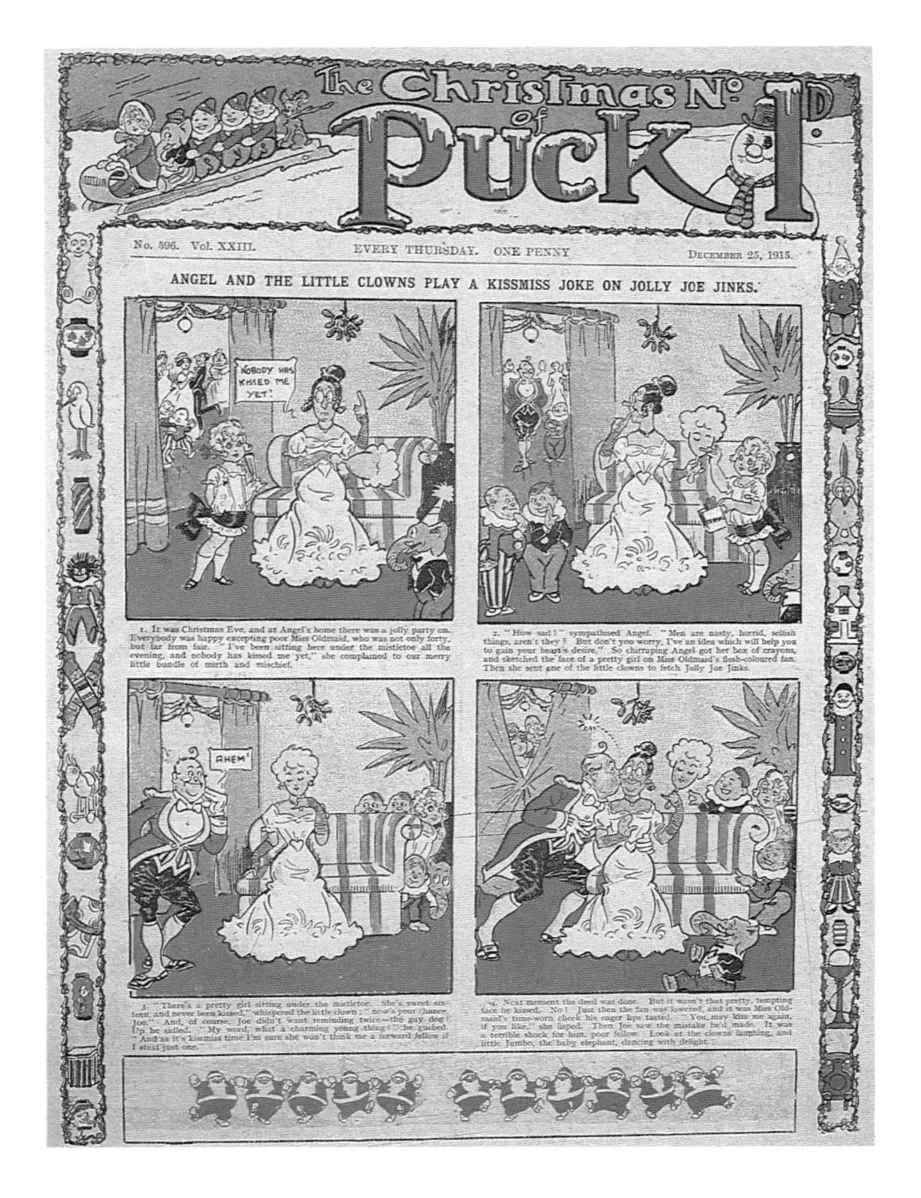
The Christmas No. of Puck 1D.
No. 596. Vol. XXIII. EVERY THURSDAY. ONE PENNY DECEMBER 25, 1915.
ANGEL AND THE LITTLE CLOWNS PLAY A KISSMISS JOKE ON JOLLY JOE JINKS.
NOBODY HAS KISSED ME YET!
1. It was Christmas Eve, and at Angel's home there was a jolly party on. Everybody was happy excepting poor Miss Oldmaid, who was not only forty, but far from fair. "I've been sitting here under the mistletoe all the evening, and nobody has kissed me yet," she complained to our merry little bundle of mirth and mischief.
2. "How sad!" sympathised Angel. "Men are nasty, horrid, selfish things, aren't they? But don't you worry, I've an idea which will help you to gain your heart's desire." So chirruping Angel got her box of crayons, and sketched the face of a pretty girl on Miss Oldmaid's flesh-coloured fan. Then she sent one of the little clowns to fetch Jolly Joe Jinks.
AHEM!
3. "There's a pretty girl sitting under the mistletoe. She's sweet sixteen, and never been kissed," whispered the little clown; "now's your chance, Joe." And, of course, Joe didn't want reminding twice—the gay dog! Up he sidled. "My word, what a charming young thing!" he gushed. "And as it's kissmiss time I'm sure she won't think me a forward fellow if I steal just one."
4. Next moment the deed was done. But it wasn't that pretty, tempting face he kissed. No! Just then the fan was lowered, and it was Miss Oldmaid's time-worn cheek his eager lips tasted. "You may kiss me again, if you like," she lisped. Then Joe saw the mistake he'd made. It was a terrible shock for him, poor fellow. Look at the clowns laughing, and little Jumbo, the baby elephant, dancing with delight.

A Fine New Floating School Story: ST. ROSA'S AT SEA. Full of Fun and Thrilling Adventure. Just Starting.

No. 37.] **CAPTAIN SKITTLE AND BOSSY THE BOS'N ARE IN A PROPER FIX!** [June 29th, 1935.

1. "The weather looks like changing, so I think I'll do the same," declared Cap'n Skittle. And in a brace of shakes he was struggling with a clean collar, trying to get it on chummy terms with his neck. But it was a tough task, he found, and suddenly the stud flew out—zip!

2. Of course, that annoyed the skipper of the *Snorter* greatly. But what made him still more cross was the fact that when he started searching for the stud he couldn't see a sign of it anywhere. The reason being, as you no doubt noticed, that Doodah, the merry dogfish, had got it.

3. Yes, it had whizzed right into his mouth. But he kept mum about it and enjoyed the spectacle of Skittle and Bossy searching high and low for that strayed stud. "'Tisn't under here!" cried Bossy, as he unwound the coil of rope. "Well, it must be somewhere!" snapped Skittle.

4. "Very helpful, aren't you?" cried Bossy. "Fancy making all this fuss about a lost collar stud! Why don't you use another one?" But Skittle gave a snort. "Don't be a chump!" he growled as he climbed up the funnel. "Whoever heard of a man with more than one stud?"

5. Well, a squint down the funnel showed no signs of the thing. And Cap'n Skittle quite overlooked the fact that the funnel was one of the tip-up variety. It swung down under his weight, and probably owing to the fact that Bossy was pushing a weeny bit too heftily with the mop.

6. "Steady, there, !" howled Skittle. "Reverse your engines!" But it was too late—the damage was done. Yes, the skipper went crashing head-first clean through the roof of the hatchway, wrenching the funnel right off. Overboard it went. "And all for a stud!" cried Bossy.

7. "S'pose I'd better rescue the captain first, although the funnel's more use! Kimmup, skipper!" With which he grabbed the yelling Skittle firmly round the starboard ankle and gave a terrific heave. That did the trick!

8. A portion of hatch came clean away, and Cap'n Skittle rose up with it. Bossy went down with a useful sort of bump, right on the hole where the funnel used to reside. He had to remain there, warm as it was, for he got fixed.

9. Down behind him on deck went Cap'n Skittle with a thud, wearing a hatch round his neck. And the sight made Doodah laugh so much that he coughed up the stud. "Well, would you believe it!" gasped Skittle. "He'd got it!"

Opposite
Freddie Flip and Uncle Bunkle were replaced in turn by Captain Skittle and Bossy the Bos'n for some lively slapstick aboard the good tub, Snorter.
© Fleetway Publications, London, 1989.

The story behind this *Radio Fun* Annual cover is that the main star was originally intended to be Tommy Handley of ITMA fame. Brown's original cover art had shown the famous comedian in the centre position and when it was announced that Handley had died, he was asked to produce a completely new drawing replacing Tommy Handley with Wilfred Pickles. This was done with considerable haste: it had fewer characters and is less detailed. The Pickles version was then used for the 1950 Annual. But a small number of Handley editions are known to exist. Needless to say, all are collector's items.
© Fleetway Publications, London, 1989.

20
T.V. FUN
February 13th, 1954
DIANA DECKER
THE Cutie-Queen of the T.V. SCREEN
HOW DO, MISS! I'VE CALLED TO DO YOUR T.V. REPAIRS!
SWELL! COME RIGHT IN, MR NUTT!
NOW ALL THAT NEEDS DOING IS —
ALL RIGHT, ALL RIGHT! I KNOW WHAT I'M UP TO, MISS! I'LL SOON SPOT THE TROUBLE!
BUT HONEY —
NOW LOOK, MISS! I DON'T TELL YOU YOUR JOB, SO PLEASE DON'T TRY TO TELL ME MINE!
O.K. HONEY! YOU HAVE IT YOUR WAY!
GOOD! NOW I CAN GET ON!
AN HOUR LATER...
IT'S QUEER, MISS, BUT I'VE TAKEN YOUR SET RIGHT DOWN AND I CAN'T FIND A THING WRONG WITH IT!
I'M NOT SURPRISED, HONEY! I WAS TRYING TO TELL YOU —
— THAT I ONLY WANTED YOU TO TIGHTEN MY AERIAL!
WELL, MR NUTT, I HAVE TO GO OUT FOR A FEW HOURS, BUT YOU WILL SEE ME AGAIN BEFORE YOU GO!
HO HO I WON'T, MISS! I'LL BE FINISHED IN NO TIME!
YOU CAN TAKE IT FROM ME THAT I SHAN'T SEE YOU AGAIN UNTIL TOMORROW WHEN I COME ROUND WITH THE BILL!
I GUESS YOU KNOW ALL THE ANSWERS, HONEY!
SEE HER AGAIN BEFORE I GO INDEED! SAUCY YOUNG THING! HOW LONG DOES SHE THINK I TAKE TO DO A JOB?
DETERMINED TO PROVE OUR DIANA WRONG, MR. NUTT COMPLETES HIS TASK IN RECORD TIME!
THAT'S THE TICKET! NOW I'LL JUST TEST FOR RECEPTION!
WELL, HELLO THERE!!!
WOW! SHE WAS RIGHT!

16
T.V. FUN
January 21st, 1956
SHIRLEY EATON
The Modern Miss — in Merry Moments
YOU LOOK FED UP, ED.! WHAT'S WRONG?
I'M HAVING TROUBLE WITH MY SCOOP STORY ON MONSIEUR PARBON, THE FAMOUS T.V. CHEF, SHIRLEY!
EDITOR
HE'S THE CHAP WHO IS SO FADDY ABOUT FOOD, BUT I CAN'T FIND OUT WHAT HIS FAVOURITE DISH IS!
THEN I'LL SEE IF I CAN INTERVIEW HIM AT THE T.V. STUDIOS!
AND SO, A MOMENT LATER...
MONSIEUR PARBON? SORRY, MISS, BUT HE'S BUSY!
OH! I'LL HAVE TO GET MY INFORMATION ELSEWHERE!
T.V. STUDIO
AH! LUCKY I SPOTTED THIS! STEAK AND CHIPS MUST BE M'SIEUR'S FAVOURITE DISH! I MUST MAKE A NOTE OF IT!
Steak and Chips for me says.. Monsieur Parbon.
with Soggs Sauce of course!
NOW I'LL POP ROUND THIS HOARDING AND BACK TO THE EDITOR!
You can't beat a nice chop says Monsieur Parbon
Especially with Podds Peas!
GOODNESS! HERE HE IS AGAIN ON THIS SIDE! SO HE LIKES CHOPS, TOO!
S'CUSE ME, MISS, BUT I'VE GOT TO STICK ANOTHER POSTER OVER THAT ONE!
THAT'S ALL RIGHT — I'VE FINISHED!
OH, NOT AGAIN! GOSH! IT STRIKES ME M'SIEUR PARBON LIKES THE LOT!
There's nothing like Roast Chicken says Monsieur Parbon. Providing you have Stodges Stuffing!
IF ONLY I KNEW HIS FAVOURITE DISH! IF HE EATS ALL THESE MEALS IN ONE DAY I RECKON HE SUFFERS FROM TUMMY PAINS!
BEEFO
FOR STRENGTH
I'M RIGHT — HE DOES!
I'm never without my MACBEANS TUMMY TABLETS SAYS Monsieur Parbon
GOSH! THINKING OF ALL THAT FOOD HAS MADE ME HUNGRY! I'LL POP INTO THIS LITTLE PLACE AND HAVE A BITE! I'M AFRAID IT WOULDN'T BE GRAND ENOUGH FOR M'SIEUR PARBON!
JEEPERS! THERE HE IS — BUYING SOMETHING, TOO!
OPEN
OUR SHIRLEY IS IN LUCK'S WAY! SHE NOT ONLY CHATS TO MONSIEUR PARBON ABOUT FOOD, BUT HE ALSO ESCORTS HER BACK TO THE OFFICE OF THE DAILY DEKKO!
WELL, ED, I'VE FOUND OUT WHAT MONSIEUR PARBON'S FAVOURITE DISH IS, BUT I AM AFRAID IT'S IN ALL THE NEWSPAPERS ALREADY!
ALL THE NEWSPAPERS?
DAILY DEKKO
YES — IT'S FISH AND CHIPS!!
(Make a date with Shirley Eaton! She will be here again in another funny episode, next Monday! Order T.V. FUN, NOW!)

Reproductions of original artwork by Brown for his weekly 12-picture set of Frank Randle (1901–57), the Lancashire music-hall comedian who appeared in several films in the Forties and Fifties – hence his inclusion in *Film Fun*. In this sequence Randall is dreaming as he sleepwalks. Note how well Brown has executed his background scenes.
© Fleetway Publications, London, 1989.

Opposite
Here's Brown in fine form with a duo of lovely ladies. Both appeared on the back page of *TV Fun* in 1954.
© Fleetway Publications, London, 1989.

G. W. WAKEFIELD

Opposite
A fine illustration by Bill Wakefield for the title-block heading of the weekly *Butterfly* comic which was issued 1904–40. This example is dated 1915 and features one of his favourite 'flappers'. Below the *Butterfly* title are two single-picture comic panels by Wakefield from a regular weekly back page feature; the latter is from a Christmas Number of the First World War. Naturally, 'the gallant lad in khaki' beats the 'johnnies in evening dress' for her attentions.
© Fleetway Publications, London, 1989.

There are few examples of sons following their fathers into the comic art profession. A notable exception, however, was George Wakefield and his son, Terry. Wakefield senior was one of the foremost British comic artists between the wars. Terry Wakefield, whose style was sometimes virtually indistinguishable from that of his father, followed faithfully in his footsteps and their work, which appeared jointly in the comic papers for around 50 years, was looked upon with affection and admiration by millions.

George William Wakefield ('Bill' or 'Billy' to almost everyone who knew him) was born in Hoxton, London on 13 November 1887. Educated locally, his early aim in life was to be a cabinet maker – an ambition soon forgotten when he won a scholarship to the Camberwell School of Arts and Crafts around 1903 and discovered his talent for drawing. He began to submit cartoon jokes to the comic papers of the time, was published in *Ally Sloper's Half Holiday* in 1906 and appeared regularly in *Scraps* and other James Henderson publications from 1907. In that year, too, he married Anne Cordwell, a young woman who lived close by (but no relation to Fred Cordwell with whom he was to be closely associated later in life).

His first comic set or strip, as opposed to the single-picture jokes he had been submitting to *Ally Sloper's* and the Henderson papers, was 'Baron De Cuft and the Hon. Samuel Shiney' and appeared in *The Comic Companion*, a short-lived (1908–09) pull-out supplement to the magazine *You and I*.

A later introduction to Fred Cordwell at the Amalgamated Press led to other commissions. Cordwell was the editor of several comic papers, including *Merry & Bright* and *The Favourite Comic*, which had commenced publication in 1910 and 1911 respectively. Bill Wakefield's work was soon appearing in both comics: two early sets he drew for Cordwell were 'Gertie Goodsort' (*Merry & Bright*: 1911) and 'Flossie and Phyllis' (*The Favourite Comic*: 1914), illustrating the amusing adventures of pretty young women – or 'flappers' as they were then termed. It was on 30 June 1911, that his only son, Terry, was born.

Wakefield was more than simply a 'funnies' artist: he had the ability to tackle serious subjects too. As early as 1910 he had been commissioned to depict the lying-in-state of King Edward VII for a leading national magazine. It was an exceptional task and one of which he spoke proudly in later years. Aware of the range of Wakefield's art, Cordwell asked him to illustrate one of the lead adventure features in his new weekly *The Penny Wonder* (1912) – a detective series called 'John Flood, the River

The Butterfly 1d.
GRAND SUMMER DOUBLE No.

No. 569. [ENTERED AT STATIONERS' HALL.] PRICE ONE PENNY. [TRANSMISSION ABROAD AT BOOK RATES.] AUGUST 7, 1915.

FLOSSIE'S ADMIRER HAD AN AWFUL S-TART!

Dear Gertie,—Aren't you looking forward to Easter? I am, awfully! You see, Cyril is playing in a big football match on Easter Monday, and, of course, I'm going to watch the game. Yesterday they had a practice match, and fine fun it was too. A bit of extra, unexpected fun turned up, apart from the game. It happened in this way. As I was standing on the touch-line, looking on, I felt somebody come up to my side. Looking round, I observed to my horror that it was Cholly Chumpleigh, that dreadful bore. I tell you, my heart sank into my boots at the mere thought of having to put up with his tedious talk for some time.. But just then a startling thing happened. One of the players kicked the ball in our direction, and it smote the tray of tarts a pastrycook's boy was carrying. Up flew the jammy dainties, clapping themselves all over Cholly's face! Those tarts must have known something, don't you think, to hide his face like that? Anyhow, it had the effect of quickly clearing him out of it. Wishing you and all a happy time this Easter. Yours merrily, FLOSSIE.

FLOSSIE CHOOSES THE PICK OF THE BUNCH.

Dear Gertie,—A merry Christmas to you, old girl! And plenty of fun with lots of nice boys. Have already had one merry evening. It was at a concert in aid of the Prince of Wales' Distress Fund, and a very nice affair it was, too, and a great success. By the way, when I drove up to the hall, judge of my surprise to find a row of johnnies in evening dress waiting for me. Each had a large bouquet ready to present to me. But at the end of the line was a gallant lad in khaki. He, too, had some flowers, but only a small bunch. But I ignored all the others, and walking straight up to the soldier, accepted his offering with a sweet smile. I didn't say anything to the other fellows, but the look I gave them—well, I shouldn't be at all surprised to hear that they have all enlisted since! With every good wish again for a merry Christmas. Yours seasonably, FLOSSIE.

Film Fun (below) was launched on 20 January 1920. The Amalgamated Press, and editor Fred Cordwell, had been influenced by the popularity of Charlie Chaplin, the front page star of *The Funny Wonder*. Bill Wakefield's style was immediately 'right' for *Film Fun*, the world's first comic devoted to the cinema. These two pages (from the first issue) are typical of his early work: a masterly depiction in 'portrait' form of Ben Turpin and Chester Conklin for the title illustration (*bottom left*) and a less formal – but equally good – version of the two comedians in comic format (*opposite*). © Fleetway Publications, London, 1989.

Twenty Big Pages and a Plate of "FATTY" ARBUCKLE.

No. 1. Vol. 1. **January 17, 1920.**

14 FILM FUN. January 17th, 1920.

Ben Turpin And Charlie Conklin

Heroes of the Paramount Mack Sennett Comedies

This Week's Comedy: "THEIR 'TAKING' LITTLE WAYS."

1. Ben and Charlie had a little picture show of their own, but the merchant who ran one over the road was getting all the patrons. Signor Softsoap, his name was, and he sang ballads which brought tears to the eyes, and bobs to the box-office. Great success he was, too. So Ben said to Charlie: "We'd better shut up, old son. He's got it all!" "Indeed, indeed, you are right, boy," replied Charlie: "What *can* we do against this competition?" "I give it up, me old trout," mournfully moaned Ben. "Let's shut down, and shut up, and hop it. I'm fed up with everything—bar grub!" And they decided to close the prems., and wander forth into the cruel, cold world.

2. So sadly and sorrowfully, Charlie shoved the key into the keyhole and sad of heart they were, and no error, till suddenly old Ben's hat fell off, so amazing was the inspiration that had got him abaft the scheme-box. "Charlie, old chunk, I've got it!" said he. "Let us e'en buy a small but choice bouquet of bedelias and book front seats at old wotsisname's show." "Right, laddie, again," replied the cheerful Charles: "Here goes the last bob for a bunch of blossoms!" And off went the two tried and trusty pals to the florists, where little Lottie made them up an extra bunch of assorted blooms and blossoms. Then off to the rival show, at the double, my lads!

3. So here were these two friendly old filberts, *well* in the front row of the stalls. And all was quite quiet and absolutely O.K., and all cheerio, till old Softsoap came on and started to warble a jolly little humorous ballad entitled: "Ho! When Love Creeps In Your Heart," or your coal-cellar, or something. "Watch me, Charlie, boy!" says Ben.

4. Well, when the professor got to the high J, or the minor K, or something, verily his mouth resembled a coal-hole, in good sooth. Simply mar-r-vellous! So then old Ben got going, and he buzzed the bouquet with remarkable precision and directness of aim. Which did it, old beans, most promptly and properly. Much to the songster's surprise, if I tell you!

Tracker'. These single illustrations to the text were strong and powerful, executed in a dark, brooding style that contributed a great deal to the mood of these tales and, of course, to their popularity.

The AP was pleased enough with the result to assign Wakefield as regular artist for the popular and long-running pre-school series 'Rook wood', written by Owen Conquest (a pseudonym of Charles Hamilton, who created Billy Bunter) which began appearing in the AP weekly *The Boys' Friend* in 1915. Unfortunately the task did not occupy him for long. The country was at war and Bill Wakefield was called up to serve in the Sixth City of London Regiment where he remained until invalided out. He returned to the comics in 1917 with another 'flapper' set entitled 'Carrie the Girl Chaplain', again for *Merry & Bright*.

All of Wakefield's comic sets were completed in pen and ink on stiff drawing card. Usually the card was in strips, with three or four pictures to a strip; on other occasions it would be cut into convenient panel sizes and there would be one drawing per piece. The young Terry Wakefield tried to emulate his father from the

5. For it copped him fairly and squarely in the cutlet-chasm, and there he was with his face full of moss-roses and tulips, and magnolias, and stuff, and trying to get out the arpeggios and bits. And the audience got up and shouted : " Ho, that's good ! That's extra, boy ! Ongcore ! Cheerio ! Do it again—we didn't quite get the first bit ! " And so forth and etc.

6. But our old pals' joy was short-lived, for a very large, naughty, massive, muscular merchant in a uniform came and grabbed our pals by their earpieces and hove them forth. And they DID come a pop, too ; and saw about 17,006,354¾ stars and stripes and spangles, while the old joint looked on at the back and cried : " Well played, Jim ! "

7. But Ben and Charlie picked each other up, and dusted each other and comforted each other, and then went back to their old home from home. And this time it was Charlie who hit on the noble notion. They got the little old apparatus all ready, and when the lights were low, they started the fun. Some experts, these bright lads, if we tell you !

8. For when the mighty multitude had rolled up outside the rival show, THEY FILMED IT ! Got a top-holeish film, too, the artful young fellows ! " This will do the trick, me priceless old parsnip," chuckled Charlie. " Now we've got them ! Now for fortune and face-feeding ! Joy, joy, boy ! Another small lemon for luck ! " And it was so.

9. Well, next evening, early, they threw the picture of the crowd on to the blank wall opposite, and, of course, all the jolly joints and dainty dames who arrived cried : " Oho ! What a crowd ! The place must be full ! Let's go into Ben and Charlie's picture palace ! " And there was Signor Softsoap turning money away from himself ! Ha, ha, ha, ha ! And Ben and Charlie rejoiced muchly, and sang of the good time coming, and so forth.

10. Well, to cut a long story fine, in about ten ticks old Ben and Charlie were sho ing up the " House Full " boards, and all was well. But old Softsoap and his trusty henchman, with the buttons, were most completely mystified and dumfoundered, and couldn't make head or tail of the business. But Ben and Charlie are still laughing and counting the takings. Bright old beans, aren't they ? Watch out for their comical capers next week.

Bumper Christmas Number!

The Boys' Friend 1½d.

No 1,020. Vol. XX. New Series.] THREE HALFPENCE. [Week Ending December 25th, 1920.

The Phantom Abbot of Rookwood!

By Owen Conquest.

MERRY CHRISTMAS! Jimmy Silver.

ALL THE BEST! Don Darrel.

GOOD FOOTER! Jack Vernon.

A BULLY HOLIDAY! Frank Richards.

1920.

THE GHOST WALKS! The juniors stood rooted to the spot, whilst the Phantom Abbot of Rookwood slowly approached them.

GREAT NEW COMPETITION! £10 in Prizes Weekly for Readers!

MERRY and BRIGHT 1½d THE FAVORITE COMIC | **COMPLETE DETECTIVE YARN** ON PAGE 7. | C

No. 198 (NEW SERIES). PRICE THREE-HALFPENCE. JANUARY 15, 1921.

1. Good-morning, all! Top of the morning to you! Here we are with a topping show for you as usual! Isn't it? Ah, there's Percy Pupp waiting for Mabel, who approaches with another bright lad. Now, Percy was standing just outside the menagerie, and the elephant was behind him, in the little pen. Watch that elephant! And see—there's good old Louise Fazenda, on a seat, doing a bit of knitting. So, finding herself short of wool, she said to Baby Marie Osborne: "Here's sixpence, dear! Get me another ball of wool!" But Marie had spotted that piece of wool hanging from the stocking of the fat joint on the end of the seat. More of that later. Hallo! Those two kids with the little sledge are about to play the merry jest on Ford Sterling! Will it come off? We shall see! And there are some more kids knocking off an old toff's topper, just as Fatty Arbuckle, who's gone in for the old clo' caper, comes round the corner. Some stunt, isn't it? Fancy our one and only Fatty taking on a job like that.

2. Well, Fatty bent to pick up a cigar-end that he'd spotted, just as the old nut's topper sailed round the corner, bang on to the other pile of hats which Fatty had on his dome. And up comes the old nut at the double to recover his crumpet-case. But, hi! Look at Ford! Yes—those kidlets bumped him all right—in fact, they sat him bang over the hole in the ice, AND THEY COULDN'T STOP THEMSELVES, as you will see in picture three. Now let's see how Baby Marie is getting on. Ha, ha! As the fat merchant ambled off, she collared the piece of worsted that stuck out of his stocking and it became unravelled—all the jolly lot of it—all in one long piece, which Baby promptly rolled into a ball. And we told you to watch that elephant, didn't we? Yoho! Look at him, raising Percy Pupp's top-hat! And mark the other chap's indignation. "Whatcher playing at?" said he.

3. "I'll show him!" cried the old chap, and he let old Percy have a swat on the snitch that completely dazzled him. Meanwhile, again we say—watch the elephant! He's put Percy's top hat on! Did ye ever! Well, well! Now to return to Baby Marie. She presented that ball of wool to Louise, who said: "Oh, you were quick, dear! Here's a penny for you for being so quick!" All right for Baby Marie, wasn't it? Very ALL right! No wonder that the fat joint in the stockings—or, rather, in the ONE stocking—began to sneeze! And now let us look at Ford, who, standing on the ice, remarked to the little lads, who'd gone in splosh: "That was a good joke, wasn't it, boys? An EXCELLENT joke! Ha, ha!" But answer there came none. But along came old Fatty, puffing at the cigar and wearing the old toff's topper. And the old toff—whoho! He was well mystified! And that'll be all till next week, peoples, when we're showing another special programme! Just a word in your ear: order your copy now.

Bill Wakefield illustrated the 'Rookwood' stories which were written for *The Boy's Friend* by Charles Hamilton, using the pseudonym Owen Conquest. This illustration (*opposite*) for the front page of the Bumper Christmas Number of 1920 is especially rare as Wakefield was pleased enough with his work to sign it. Hamilton's tales of Rookwood School developed a huge following, as did his 'Greyfriars' stories for the popular weekly story paper *The Magnet* for which he wrote as Frank Richards. © Fleetway Publications, London, 1989.

Bill Wakefield's enthusiasm for the silent cinema spilled over into another comic paper under Fred Cordwell's control: *Merry & Bright* (*above*). Here he has managed to incorporate several of the stars he was drawing for *Film Fun* . The pen and ink originals of these drawings would have measured approximately 36 cm × 10 cm high, not an easy area to fill. Wakefield managed it beautifully, however, creating an absorbing front page. He was also responsible for the two title headings. © Fleetway Publications, London, 1989.

8 SPORTS' FUN February 11, 1922

Don't miss " My Funniest Experience on the Field," by S. C. Puddefoot, on page 4.

Next Week's Cartoon: " Useful Training Hints," by Harold Gough, Sheffield United and English international.

February 11, 1922 SPORTS' FUN 5

This Cartoon cannot fail to amuse you. No. 2, SPORTS' FUN,

Next week's Cartoon: "Some 'Notes' on Footballers Before the Footlights," by George Wilson, of Sheffield Wednesday and English international.

Wakefield was a keen sports fan and took particular pleasure in his commissions for a new AP weekly, *Sports Fun*, started by his friend and editor, Fred Cordwell, in 1922. The now almost forgotten sporting personalities shown here were depicted by Wakefield in the same style as he was now using for *Film Fun*, the new cinema weekly which had commenced publication two years before.
© Fleetway Publications, London, 1989.

Even beneath his coatings of tar and feathers, the character here being afforded such rough treatment is easily recognisable as Harry Langdon, the baby-faced star of silent film comedies made in the 1920s. Wakefield drew Langdon for *The Kinema Comic* during the late Twenties and early Thirties. The original pen and ink drawings are a huge 22 cm × 15 cm.
© Fleetway Publications, London, 1989.

Opposite
The Sparkler was a tabloid weekly which began publication in 1934. Bill Wakefield's first work for the comic was a not particularly noteworthy set entitled 'Chubby and Chirpy'; he improved upon this considerably, however, in the following year when he was asked to supply 'Here There and Everywhere', also known as 'Freddie Flip and Uncle Bunkle', a 10-picture feature for an inside page. Wakefield obviously enjoyed his two characters and their travels around the world, as shown by this example involving an aeroplane show and some sticky hot toffee. But clearly he was not as happy with the more 'comic' style of drawing as he was with either a 'straight' style or that used for *Film Fun*.
© Fleetway Publications, London, 1989.

age when he could first hold a pencil, using off-cuts from his father's materials. Soon his father started drawing things for Terry to copy and later taught him how to 'animate' the drawings, fostering the artist's techniques that injected life into each panel. It was all training that was to serve him in good stead in later years.

For many years Bill Wakefield indulged in a somewhat uncommon pastime for an artist: seemingly oblivious to the possibility of damaging his drawing hand, he was an active amateur boxer and a frequent participant at fairground exhibition matches where members of the audience would be invited to climb into the ring to fight the current champion for a cash sum for each round fought, or for an outright win. According to Terry Wakefield, prize money was not always forthcoming, but this never daunted his father, who donned his gloves for sheer enjoyment.

By 1920 the cinema was so well

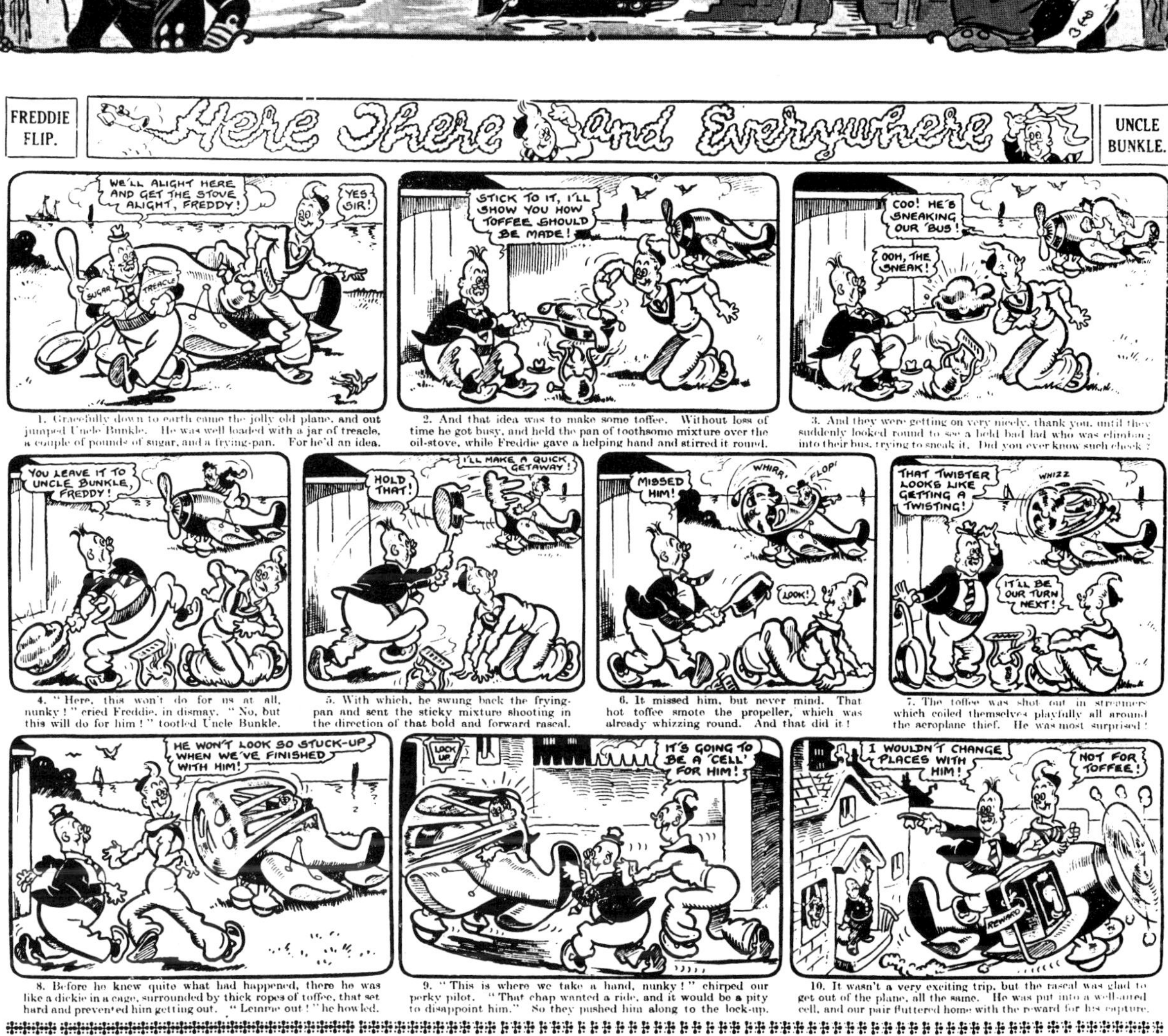

established that Fred Cordwell and his employers at the AP combined films with comics to come up with a new and, eventually, famous weekly – *Film Fun*. It was so successful that Cordwell within a few weeks launched a companion entitled *The Kinema Comic*. Both titles were perfectly suited to Bill Wakefield's abilities, a fact obvious to Cordwell from the start; so much so that he instructed all artists working on the two papers to copy Wakefield's style, right down to the lettering in the word-balloons!

Wakefield's forte was in depicting perfect likenesses of people, which

LARRY SEMON APPEARS THIS WEEK ON PAGE 23

No. 358. Vol. 7. March 5th, 1927.

THE SCHOLARSHIP BOY'S WONDERFUL WIN!

Like lightning his fist shot out and caught Topperton a smashing thud on the chin that caused him to give a curious gasp and then go flat on his back. "Eight—nine—ten—out!" yelled the referee. "Hamilton's the winner!" *(See page 2.)*

When *Film Fun* was launched on 17 January 1920, its success was evident within weeks. Cordwell and the Amalgamated Press then followed standard practice – creating their own competition in the form of a similar publication, thus leaving little scope for other publishers to follow suit. The result in this case was *The Kinema Comic*, launched on 24 April 1920. Once again Wakefield was the premier artist, depicting then-famous but now nearly forgotten personalities such as Ford Sterling, Larry Semon and Walter Forde. His best-known regular feature was 'Fatty Arbuckle' which was quickly discontinued after a Hollywood scandal had made the fat comedian unacceptable. Compared to *Film Fun*, the *Kinema* had a relatively short run of 12 years. The front pages shown here are all by Bill Wakefield.
© Fleetway Publications, London, 1989.

made him ideal for *Film Fun* and *Kinema Comic*: both featured picture strip adventures of the stars of the cinema looking just as they did on the silver screen. His drawings were never caricatures but managed to capture the natural characteristics of his subjects. He was so skilled that, like Herbert Foxwell and his drawings of comic animals, he was in a class of his own.

Bill Wakefield would sometimes journey to a cinema up to 50 miles away to see a particular character to be depicted in *Film Fun* or in an illustration for a story in Cordwell's subsequent *Film Picture Stories*. If the films were not available he would use black and white still photographs to obtain the likeness he wanted. Terry Wakefield was later to work in the same way.

At the age of 14 Terry became his father's full-time assistant. His job was to rule up panel sizes, clean the completed drawings by rubbing out pencil marks, ink-in areas of black where necessary and, whenever possible, practise the techniques his father taught him. Later, Terry attended Richmond Art School and,

The Bullseye (1931–4) was one of the most exciting story papers ever to be published by the AP. It is now much sought by collectors. The stories were always dramatic and often fresh in their approach. It is clear that editor Fred Cordwell had some excellent writers working for him (although the stories were always anonymous). One of these was known to be Alfred Edgar who created 'The House of Thrills' serial (see title heading above) and later wrote for the theatre and films with enormous success. Another was Cordwell himself. The illustrations on these two pages show the range of Wakefield's art and how good he was at 'straight' illustration. The depiction of the Chinaman to the right is quite masterly.
© Fleetway Publications, London, 1989.

Secrets of the Silent Thames and its Watchful Guardians—The River Police!

FROM THE SECRET PLACES OF LONDON'S CHINATOWN THE TENTACLES OF THE TONG OF THE RED SHADOW SPREAD UP AND DOWN THE THAMES. SOFT-FOOTED CHINESE FLIT LIKE GHOSTS AMONGST THE BLACK WHARVES, MENACING THE WAREHOUSES AND PILFERING STORES, DEMANDING TOLL OF ALL WHO USE THE RIVER. LIKE SOME VENGEFUL HAWK, THE BLACK LAUNCH OF THE NIGHT PATROL PURSUES THEM, LED BY NICK KENNEDY. HE ALONE OF ALL MEN HAS LOOKED UPON THE EVIL FEATURES OF FANG-WU, THE LEADER OF THE RED SHADOW TONG, AS YOU WILL LEARN IN THIS THRILLING STORY, ENTITLED: "THE TONG OF THE RED SHADOW."

There came a terrific crash as the bottom of the van hit the road's edge. Then it bucked high, and tilted forward. Nick Kennedy saw the policeman flung out, then he himself was shot from his seat. He grabbed wildly at the side of the van, but felt it falling with him.

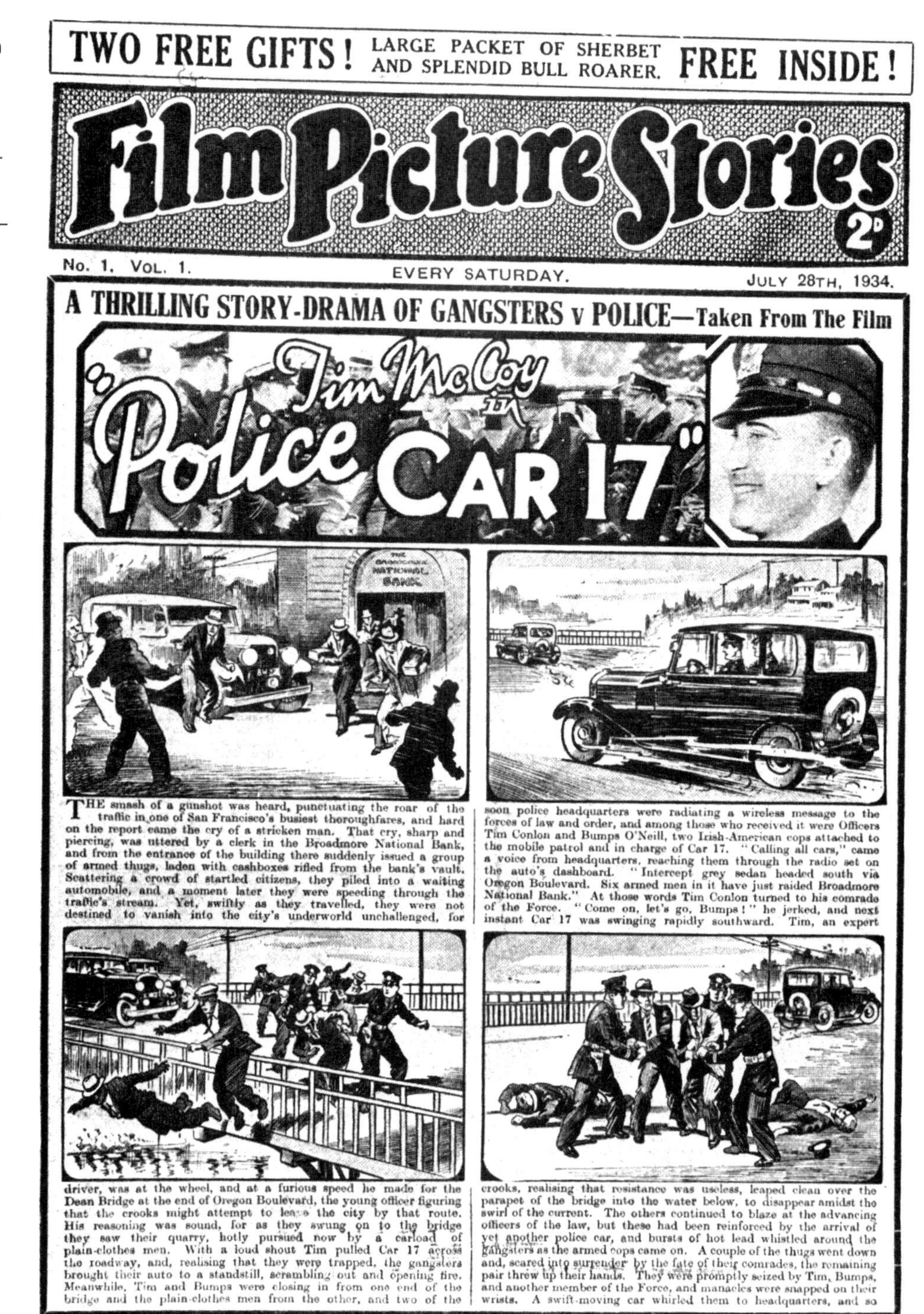

TWO FREE GIFTS! LARGE PACKET OF SHERBET AND SPLENDID BULL ROARER. FREE INSIDE!

Film Picture Stories

2d

No. 1, Vol. 1. EVERY SATURDAY. July 28th, 1934.

A THRILLING STORY-DRAMA OF GANGSTERS v POLICE—Taken From The Film

Tim McCoy in "Police Car 17"

THE smash of a gunshot was heard, punctuating the roar of the traffic in one of San Francisco's busiest thoroughfares, and hard on the report came the cry of a stricken man. That cry, sharp and piercing, was uttered by a clerk in the Broadmore National Bank, and from the entrance of the building there suddenly issued a group of armed thugs, laden with cashboxes rifled from the bank's vault. Scattering a crowd of startled citizens, they piled into a waiting automobile, and a moment later they were speeding through the traffic's stream. Yet, swiftly as they travelled, they were not destined to vanish into the city's underworld unchallenged, for soon police headquarters were radiating a wireless message to the forces of law and order, and among those who received it were Officers Tim Conlon and Bumps O'Neill, two Irish-American cops attached to the mobile patrol and in charge of Car 17. "Calling all cars," came a voice from headquarters, reaching them through the radio set on the auto's dashboard. "Intercept grey sedan headed south via Oregon Boulevard. Six armed men in it have just raided Broadmore National Bank." At those words Tim Conlon turned to his comrade of the Force. "Come on, let's go, Bumps!" he jerked, and next instant Car 17 was swinging rapidly southward. Tim, an expert driver, was at the wheel, and at a furious speed he made for the Dean Bridge at the end of Oregon Boulevard, the young officer figuring that the crooks might attempt to leave the city by that route. His reasoning was sound, for as they swung on to the bridge they saw their quarry, hotly pursued now by a carload of plain-clothes men. With a loud shout Tim pulled Car 17 across the roadway, and, realising that they were trapped, the gangsters brought their auto to a standstill, scrambling out and opening fire. Meanwhile, Tim and Bumps were closing in from one end of the bridge and the plain-clothes men from the other, and two of the crooks, realising that resistance was useless, leaped clean over the parapet of the bridge into the water below, to disappear amidst the swirl of the current. The others continued to blaze at the advancing officers of the law, but these had been reinforced by the arrival of yet another police car, and bursts of hot lead whistled around the gangsters as the armed cops came on. A couple of the thugs went down and, scared into surrender by the fate of their comrades, the remaining pair threw up their hands. They were promptly seized by Tim, Bumps, and another member of the Force, and manacles were snapped on their wrists. A swift-moving car whirled them to headquarters, and so

Another new weekly from Cordwell was *Film Picture Stories* which commenced when *The Bullseye* was discontinued. It was unsuccessful and had a remarkably short run of less than seven months (July 1934–February 1935). Each issue adapted several recent films into strip form and Wakefield was commissioned to draw one of these per week. His references were the film itself (he was occasionally given a private showing) or black and white stills obtained for him by Fred Cordwell. © Fleetway Publications, London, 1989.

while he was there, the elder Wakefield showed some of his work to H. J. Garrish, the director in charge of the comics at the AP. Garrish liked what he saw and offered Terry a position on the staff at Fleetway House. He started work in 1927 for editor Langton Townley and his first published work was for the nursery comic *Tiny Tots*.

In the meantime, Bill Wakefield was fully occupied turning out scores of sets for *Film Fun* and *Kinema Comic*. He drew most of the main silent stars throughout the 1920s including Babe Marie Osborne, Mack Swain, Ben Turpin and Charlie Conklin, Jackie Coogan and Grock the Clown. But it was on 8 November 1930, at the dawn of sound cinema, that Wakefield had published the first of what was to become his classic series: 'Laurel and Hardy'. Initially appearing in the centre pages, the

July 28th, 1934. FILM PICTURE STORIES. 3

The following morning Big Bill Standish, alias Dr. Madison, had occasion to try out his disguise on one of his former henchmen—none other than Johnny Davis, who ran a garage as a cloak to his lawless activities. "Well, Davis," said Standish, entering the youngster's office, "you certainly bungled that Broadmore Bank job." With a scared exclamation, Johnny snatched out a gun, but, curtly ordering him to lay it aside, the disguised gaol-bird revealed his true identity. Then he proceeded to relate his plans—plans for a big jewel robbery, which was to be followed by the kidnapping of Lieutenant Regan. "Your friendship with the Regans might help us there, Johnny," he finished. Alive to the fact that Lieutenant Regan was in jeopardy so long as Standish was at large, the police made every effort to trace the racketeer during the next few days, but some clue to his whereabouts had still to be discovered when the chief of the force, Captain Hart, dropped in at the crippled officer's home one evening. "Don't worry," he said. "It's common knowledge that Standish has sworn to get you, but there's a strong cordon of the boys from headquarters around your house." Whereupon Regan smiled dryly. "Take them away—let Standish come for me—it may prove his undoing," he counselled, but Hart refused to risk the lieutenant's life. About that same time, in his office at the garage, Johnny Davis and three more of Standish's hirelings were setting their watches in preparation

for the jewel robbery which their leader had planned. "The boss won't figure in the play," Johnny said, "but he's gauged everything for us, right down to the last detail. Now we've got to make every connection right on the dot, and the job will be carried out per schedule. The hands on my watch stand at seven-ten. You fellows adjust yours to ten minutes past seven as well." This was done, and then the crooks separated, Johnny driving up-town to the Assembly Rooms, where a masque ball was being held. Johnny was attired in the uniform of a fire-brigade chief, for the dance was a fancy-dress affair. He had arranged to meet Helen there, and found her waiting in the annexe, decked out in a Spanish costume. They danced together a good deal, and in the course of conversation Helen mentioned that her father was to go to hospital in the morning for an operation which, he hoped, would give him back the use of his legs. It was immediately after she had made this remark that Standish accosted Johnny, the escaped gaol-bird being dressed as a cardinal. Standish requested the pleasure of a dance with Helen, giving the younger man a chance to slip away unnoticed. In a certain jewellery store not far away, the other three ruffians in Standish's pay were rifling the contents of a strong-room, but one of the gangsters was careless, and knocked over a telephone that was standing on the edge of a desk. As the receiver of the instrument fell from its hook, communication was automatically

established between the store and the district telephone exchange. "You bungling fool, Spike, do you want to land us all in gaol!" snapped the thug, who was nearest to the fellow who had capsized the phone, and those fierce words came over the wire to one of the girl operators at the exchange. The operator was a quick-thinking young woman, and the moment she had found out whence those words had come, she plugged in on the switchboard and made contact with police headquarters. "There's something wrong at Fabian's Jewel Store, on State Street," she reported, and within thirty seconds a radio message was being sent out from the station to the police car that was patrolling the area in which the Fabian building was situated. It was Car 17, and Tim and Bumps O'Neill instantly drove towards the store at full speed, swinging into State Street exactly one minute after the wireless set on the auto's dashboard had picked up the call from headquarters. And as they careered in the direction of the jewellery establishment the two officers saw the thieves diving out of the premises and scrambling into a closed car standing at the kerb. "There go our men, Bumps!" yelled Tim. "We've caught 'em red-handed!" But he spoke too soon, for the gangsters had taken the alarm, and before the mobile cops could bear down on them the closed car was storming away from the scene of the robbery. "Straight for the corner of 17th Street and Douglas Avenue, Slim," one of the

series became so popular that Fred Cordwell was soon obliged to move it to the front and back pages of *Film Fun*, where the two comedians remained for more than 25 years.

The likenesses of Oliver Hardy and Stan Laurel were exact. No one has ever drawn them better. Wakefield perfectly captured the large, bulky, yet somehow graceful, figure of Oliver Hardy with his black locks of hair drooping down on to his forehead and the thin, often tearful Stan, invariably getting Olly into 'another fine mess'.

During the 1930s Bill Wakefield's regular weekly sets included 'Joe E. Brown', 'Wheeler & Woolsey', 'Max Miller', 'Lupino Lane' and 'George Formby'. Formby, in particular, was Wakefield at his best. This set, together with 'Laurel and Hardy', is generally acknowledged as his finest work.

Wakefield's forte was in the careful and accurate likenesses he drew for *Film Fun*. He excelled at the single-page 8-picture or double-page 15-picture comic adventures of the big names of silent and sound cinema. This page shows some of his work from the late Twenties and early Thirties. ('Grock' was Adrien Wettach, a Swiss clown who made several silent films in Britain and whom Wakefield drew in 1929.) The following pages show Wakefield's work at its best in the Golden Age of the late 1930s.

© Fleetway Publications, London, 1989.

GRAND CHRISTMAS WEEK NUMBER!

Film Fun 2d.

No. 780. Vol. 15. Every Tuesday. December 29th, 1934.

LAUREL AND HARDY. This Week: MISUNDERSTOOD!

THE FAMOUS FUNNY FELLOWS OF THE FILMS!

1. It was a brisk evening round about Christmas, and there was Stan Laurel out for a toddle round on his ownsome. Suddenly he spotted the brightly-lit shop. "Aha!" he gurgled, pulling up. "That reminds me." With which words, inside he went.

2. Now not far behind, strange to say, was dear old Olly Hardy. And when he reached the emporium, he, too, was smitten with a sudden notion. "Mashed macaroni!" he cried. "I was nearly forgetting and that would never do!" So inside the shop he toddled.

3. They didn't see one another, and Stan went straight home with the box he had under his arm. He looked jolly pleased with himself, too. But even as he placed that parcel on the table, in burst Olly, likewise loaded. "What's in that box?" asked Stan.

4. Which was a perfectly natural question to ask, was it not? Quite harmless. But it started a whole basinful of bother. For Olly replied: "Aha! Wouldn't you like to know?" Now this got Stan's goat. "No need to make such a mystery of it!" he yapped.

5. Then Olly pointed to the box on the table. "What have you got in there?" he asked, being curious. But Stan was not going to satisfy his inquisitiveness on that point. "You find out!" he snapped. "That's my business, so mind your own interference."

6. Whereupon the smile slithered off Olly's face. "Oh, so that's your nasty little temper, is it?" he cried. "Well, I'll soon show you. I don't care what's inside the rotten thing! Some rubbish, I'll be bound. Anyway, clear it off. I want to put my box there!"

7. As he spoke, he gave Stan's purchase a slam that sent it flying, and it bounced on to the floor. "Hoi! Be careful!" yelled Stan wrathfully. "What d'you think you're playing at?" But Olly slammed his box down. *(Continued on page 24.)*

4 GRAND FREE GIFTS FOR YOU!

SEE PAGE 21.

No. 981. Vol. 17. Every Tuesday. November 5th, 1938.

LAUREL AND HARDY

This Week: A COUPLE OF SWELL GUYS!

1. On Bonfire Night Stan and Olly had a date with Clara, the pretty daughter of Inspector Coppem, and it was Olly's suggestion that they should have their likenesses taken and present them to the fair one. Here we see our couple tripping into the photographer's.

2. Then our couple of beaus performed perfectly priceless poses before the camera. A pretty snappy scene, eh, folks? The photographer had had very taking ways ever since he had opened up business, and he pressed bulbs and said the jolly old deed was did.

3. In two very quick shakes of a lamb's tale that little chappie brought to light from the dark room a couple of life-size photos of our cheery chums. Stan looked in a glass and told himself that some underhanded business was going on beneath Olly's old bowler hat.

4. As it happed the lads met Clara on their way home, and the dear, sweet damsel flashed her orbs at Stan and told him that she particularly wanted to see him at the bonfire celebrations. Olly came all over jealous and realised that Clara preferred Stan.

5. Clara informed Stan that the fireworks commenced at eight pronto, but Olly meant to make sure they started before that. Whilst the damsel was telling Stan not to be present and correct until eight, Olly spotted a reward notice for Stick-em-Up Stan.

6. Little Stan toddled up as if he hadn't a care in the world, little knowing that Olly meant him to get a proper pasting. You see, our mass of merriment had stuck Stan's likeness on the poster and to all intents, as well as appearances, Stan was the wanted man. And Olly meant to see this came to the notice of the local constabulary.

7. When the bluebottle's optics alighted on the portrait of Stan, he gave a hop, skip, and a dive and landed on our little lump of laughter's back. Stan was quite overcome by this introduction to the hefty man-in-blue, and he kissed the pavement. As he did so he noticed his features on the poster. ***(Continued on page 24.)***

Wakefield was particularly good at depicting comic policemen, as is shown in the last two pictures.
© Fleetway Publications, London, 1989.

1. Constable Copperknob had a nasty outlook on life in the shape of a face which looked as if it had been used for a doormat since an early age. As his outlook was nothing to write home about it was not surprising that he also had a heart as hard as a rock cake. He firmly refused to let the kids of the neighbourhood buy fireworks.

2. So Bert and Bob promised to lend a helping hand each and purchase the necessary whizzbangs, etc., which go to make Bonfire Night a successful evening. Bob led the way, taking charge of the proceeds, and here we see them tootling towards the nearest firework vendor's emporium. But a little upset was soon to come to them.

3. Yes, it rather upset the boys' applecart when the barrow was pushed on a trapdoor which wasn't there. The money spilled over the brim and before Bert and Bob could count how much was there it had disappeared into the depths. So they fell down on the job.

4. Bob kept hold of the barrow even if he dropped the contents, and he had not let go even though he realised there was no money in it. He tugged on the doings and as he brought it to pavement level something came from out the blue—a bundle of fireworks.

5. To say Bert and Bob were surprised would be stating a whole bibful. They could have collapsed with surprise, but they didn't. "This is what I call quick action and swell service!" Bert cried. "We drop the money down and the fireworks come from aloft."

6. This incident had happed in a brace of shakes, which, as you know, folks, isn't very long. The boys returned to the spot where they had left the kids to find that Copperknob, the copper with the copper nob, was still spoiling the scenery and keeping eyes on the lads.

7. Observing Bert and Bob, the nasty cop decided to put a little light on the subject. "What's in that there parcel there?" he cried. Saying which he trotted forward and held out his lamp so that he could make a thorough examination. Please note the flame from the lamp igniting the fuse of a large protruding roman candle.

8. Copperknob soon had inside information on the contents, and we're pleased to state that he burned his fingers over being so inquisitive. The ladlets thoroughly enjoyed the firework display, and if the copper had not been such a thoroughly nasty guy he would have realised he was the centre of the attraction. Cheers!

These two American comedians were favourites in the Thirties. Bob Woolsey (the bespectacled half of the duo) died in 1938, but Wakefield senior continued to draw the team for some time.
© Fleetway Publications, London, 1989.

1. 'Twas the jolly old Fifth of November and everyone was going off to buy fireworks, except our dear old friend Harold. He was short of ready, and in order to get some fireworks for his sweetie's young brother, he offered to carry home Oscar Oddfellow's collection of crackers, cannons, rockets, catherine wheels, and whizzbangs.

2. This chappie promised our lad some if he would toddle home to the other side of the town carrying the heavy case. Harold thought he would get at least a couple of bob's worth, or even fireworks to the value of two bob. But he had another guess coming when the share-out arrived. For that very mean merchant merely gave him two.

3. Too bad, eh ? Then along trotted Hyam Beefy, a fellow with muscles like sparrow's ankles, and a chest measurement of fifty-five inches in the shade. He was the sort of chappie who cracks nuts with a coke hammer and he assisted Harold out of the way.

4. Harold did not like this. In other words, he objected strongly. The strong man started to do his act which looked rather good on the strength of it. Harold had an idea and he applied a vesta to the whizzbang that kind-hearted, generous Oscar had given to him.

5. The whizzbang did its work and everything turned out according to plan. The strong man jumped with fright and his dumb-bell fell on to Oscar's dome. So Harold got his own back on the mean specimen and told himself things had not gone off so badly after all.

6. Then Oscar got tough. He was one of those chaps who don't believe in taking everything without giving something in exchange. He gave that chap back his dumb-bell with interest, and a bit more force, and then took the fence in his stride in order to get to work.

7. On the way Oscar buzzed his cigar and it fell into his box of fireworks. Needless to state the fireworks then commenced and a very merry crowd gathered round to see the double entertainment. Harold reaped in much bunce which he forthwith and straightway put in his old back pocket and toddled round to Freda's abode.

8. That night, being Bonfire Night, they visited the Firework celebrations and the sweetie's little brother had a grand time. Harold is a bright spark, isn't he, folks ? He tucked into a swell feed whilst the ladlet took a front seat. Next week your old friend appears in another screamingly funny adventure. Don't miss him !

Harold Lloyd, the star of hundreds of silent two-reelers, was drawn for several years by Bill Wakefield. On this occasion he had some help from his son, Terry, whose work had recently begun to appear in *Film Fun*. © Fleetway Publications, London, 1989.

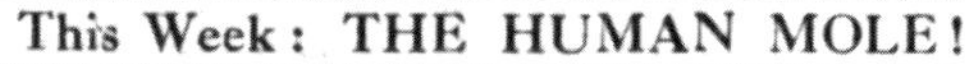

1. Howdo, Folks,—A merry Whitsun to you, and many of 'em! As for little me, well, the first post on Whit Monday brought a surprise packet. Uncle Ned, who is simply bubbling over with money, sent a note asking me to mind his twin nephews, Terence and Thomas, for the day. And, as I was reading it, the two lads breezed in.

2. Terry and Tom were a couple of real terrors, and if they didn't get what they wanted at the first time of asking they let everyone know about it. The tap-juice soon commenced to flow because they wanted to see the regatta. I soon decided to do anything they liked.

3. It was a bit of bad luck that other people, and a pretty large number of them, wanted to see the regatta besides the twins. All the ringside seats were occupied, and it was a pretty tall request to ask the kids to look over the heads of the crowd. I was flummoxed.

4. I've never been so rattled, not counting the time I took a back seat in the Old Crock's race, of course, and the thought that something had to be done weighed on the old dome like a wagonload of bricks. Then I was suddenly gifted with one of those notions you very rarely think of just when you want to. It was the solution.

5. Those kids piled on the agony as much as they could, and looked as if they would continue to do so far into the future. They made it as plain as a madeira cake, that unless they saw the regatta, Uncle Ned would hear all about it. Knowing that to fall out with my nunkie would not be welcomed from my point of view, I got to work.

6. With the aid of a barrel and a plank, I made a see-saw, and solved the prob. Seated on either end of the see-saw those kids were both able to get an eyeful of the exhibition. Life is full of ups and downs and all that, but I felt that I had settled the argument to the satisfaction of all present, including my modest self. All was well!

7. The regatta over did not see the end of my troubles, however. On the contrary, they seemed to have only just started. The kids bleated that they wanted to go to the fair, and one wants a pretty penny to go there. Your humble had not as much as change for a halfpenny, and I realised that a storm would very soon develop.

Joe E. Brown, the American film star with the over-wide mouth was a regular feature in *Film Fun* for nearly two decades. He was drawn by the elder Wakefield in the Thirties and Terry Wakefield in the Forties. © Fleetway Publications, London, 1989.

1937 was an important year for both Wakefields. Bill was at his peak, busier and better than ever; additionally *Film Fun* was given an annual, dated 1938, and he was asked to contribute the cover illustration and some original work for the interior. In each case he did a superior job and the annual is now a collector's item. It was also a landmark year for Terry, who for the first time was asked to draw Laurel and Hardy for a special booklet to be given away in *Film Fun* entitled *The Laurel and Hardy Book of Wisecracks*. In 1935 he had married Irene Gunnis (the daughter of AP artist and professional painter Louis Gunnis) and in 1938 she gave birth to their son, John. Terry's new responsibilities at home were matched by additional commitments at the AP as his experience broadened. Besides *Film Fun* he was asked to submit work to several other popular

This Week: A GREAT HIT!

1. 'Twas New Year's Day at the North Pole and the South Pole, too, and quite naturally it was also New Year's Day in the George Formby abode. Outside the snow was snowing and working overtime; inside George was in his study resolving to do others before they did him and to help others before they helped themselves.

2. Most people make a habit of making resolutions in the New Year and also make a habit of forgetting them. But not so George. As there was no chance of carrying out his resolution in the privacy of his study, he sallied fifth to search for some soul in need of help.

3. A couple of youngsters, who wished to aspire to great heights in the building trade when they grew up, were getting their hands in by erecting a snowman. Along came a rough tough, a bit of a pushful personality, and this merchant spoilt the kiddies' handiwork.

4. George realised that more than a helping hand was needed, namely a couple of closely knotted fists, and he sparred up to the bruiser. Let us mention that Ned Knockemout was tough. He could have stopped a tram with one hand, and when he came to blows with George, our lad fell over himself to get out of the way.

5. Leaving his visiting card, Ned Knockemout left by the emergency exit, and George sat up and took notice. Please note the notice and you will realise why good old George broke his resolution not to make more than one resolution. "I resolve to teach that bully a sharp lesson!" he cried. "I'll get my own back!"

6. George took up his training quarters in the well-appointed scullery of his old homestead, and Tim and Tom, the two youngsters, accepted the jobs of trainers. Tim's great-grandfather had invented a recipe to make weak men strong, and strong men stronger, and the laddie lit the copper fire in order to prepare the mixture. Our mirthquake started some strong-arm stuff with the expanders.

7. You can always rely on good old George raising a laugh, and he's not so backward at raising a pair of barbells when the occasion demands. As he was up against a pretty tough proposition he had strong reasons for wanting to get his strength above s-par. As for the two bright lads, they heated the water hot and then studied the ancient recipe to see just exactly what ingredients they required.

Jan. 7. 1939. **FILM FUN** A HAPPY NEW YEAR TO YOU ALL 9

8. The first things on the list were four pairs of extra-strong, reliable dumbbells, for, as you know, all invigorating mixture has "iron" in it. George tried various other appliances for getting his strength up, most of which we will skip, after which he hopped to it with a skipping-rope. Here we see him jumping to it in style.

9. The next ingredients for the strength-giving tonic were a trio of fenders, preferably ones made of cast-iron. These were shoved in to simmer whilst George proceeded with the good work of limbering up his muscles. George did not fancy the stew much, but he knew that unless he took it he would be in a much worse stew later

10. Here you can see a picture with a punch in it. George meant to strike for his rights, not forgetting to use his left occasionally, and made a big hit with the punchball. The kidlets were also getting on with the good work, and a goodly supply of iron filings found their way into the concoction in the copper. And if their word is anything to go by, trouble is "brewing" for Knockemout.

11. Twenty-four hours, or one whole day, after the ingredients had been placed in the copper, Tim announced that the stuff was ready for the drinking. Our laddie thought it a bit too much to swallow, but the kiddies did not mean to take no for an answer. "One dollop of this stuff," tootled Tim, "and you'll feel fit to give battle to King Kong. Take a seat and take all your medicine."

12. Poor old George took a back seat whilst the kidlets ladled the stuff out to him. Never in his life, not even in his days of sampling seaside landladies' soup, had he tasted anything so unpalatable. "You'll have an iron constitution after this little lot, Mr. Formby," said Tim. "You'll be as hard as nails." There was certainly a lot of truth in that remark, for old George felt about as fit as a fender.

13. That night was the night of the fight, and Ned Knockemout thought he was on a sure thing and that the fight was all over bar the punching. Tim and Tom had different ideas on the subject, but although they had great faith in their concoction they wanted to make absolutely certain. So, whilst one put a horseshoe in our lad's right glove, t'other filled his left glove with a pint of best cement.

14. They did this to ensure that the tough had a hard time. George led with his left, followed it with his right, and Ned Knockemout was knocked out. Yes, only three blows were exchanged. George hit the tough, then walloped him again, and the tough hit the canvas. It was much more than he could stand up for and the ref counted him out and announced that George Formby was the winner and entitled to the sum of ten quidlets. So our mirthmaker kept his resolution of lending a helping hand and made a big hit into the bargain. He's a real knockout, isn't he, folks? Having collected, he informed the kidlets that he was taking them to the panto.

15. Sydney Howard as Aladdin in "Aladdin and His Lamp," was enough to make the kiddies' faces light up, and here we see them in a box with a box of chocs each. George did not take a back seat and remained the centre of attraction. It was a great show, folks, and if you had been there you would have enjoyed it just as much as our mirthquake did. Good old George wishes *you* a Happy and Prosperous New Year and all you wish yourself. Next week he appears in another screamingly funny mirth-raiser which is the last word in laughs. Make sure of reading it, folks. It's the real goods and is entitled: "The Burning Question." So don't miss it!

Popular since his first film in 1933, it was five years before George Formby, drawn by Bill Wakefield, appeared in *Film Fun*.
© Fleetway Publications, London, 1989.

Above is a reproduction of a superb original from a George Formby set. Observe how Wakefield senior has filled the picture and how animated he has made it. His likeness of George Formby, as with all the other characters he drew, is perfect. Indeed, so good was he at getting faces 'right', that Fred Cordwell requested Wakefield to draw many of his characters' heads with a range of expressions. Cordwell then had these printed on gummed paper, passed them on to other artists when they were about to take on a Wakefield set, and instructed them to draw only the bodies. The heads would be cut from the gummed paper and stuck in the correct positions as required.
© Fleetway Publications, London, 1989.

Below is a reproduction of an original drawing which is part of a Laurel and Hardy set (original size approximately 21 cm × 9 cm). Note again how successfully Wakefield filled it with some skilful cross-hatching overall and the ever-present bollard (so common to *Film Fun* sets) to the right. The speech-balloon also helps. There were then many more words in a balloon than nowadays: the editor obviously believed that this gave good value for money. Once, Wakefield was asked to give Stan and Olly so much to say that he was obliged to have them lying on the floor with vast balloons filled with words cramming the space above. As no explanation was given to the reader for their horizontal position, the result must have been quite baffling.
© Fleetway Publications, London, 1989.

weeklies which included *Bubbles*, *Tip Top*, *Butterfly* and *Joker*.

Both Wakefields were thus fully employed turning out large quantities of artwork for what has since proved to be a golden age of comics. This was brought to an abrupt end by the Second World War. Terry was called up and served first in the Royal Artillery Anti-Aircraft as a rank gunner and, later, in the King's Own Yorkshire Light Infantry with whom he was wounded in Italy.

Bill Wakefield died suddenly at the age of 54 on 12 May 1942, while working on 'Abbott and Costello', a new set for *Film Fun*. Few realised it then, owing to the traditional anonymity of those who drew for the comic papers, but the nation had lost one of its finest draughtsmen, whose skilful penmanship and sense of humour created enjoyment for millions.

In November 1945, Terry was demobbed and immediately applied to the AP for employment. But work was difficult to come by. The comics had been hard-hit by the war, due mainly to shortage of paper and other commodities. Many weeklies had been discontinued and those that were left now appeared fortnightly and had fewer pages. However, a later visit to Fred Cordwell proved fortunate as the artist then drawing Laurel and Hardy was no longer able to do so and Terry was immediately offered the job. It was to be a long-term assignment: Terry drew the set almost continuously until the death of Oliver Hardy in 1957, soon after which it was discontinued. In addition he became the regular artist for the George Formby set which appeared for years, running concurrently with 'Laurel and Hardy' in *Film Fun*.

Throughout the 1950s he also drew 'Red Skelton', 'Peter Sellers' and 'Tony Hancock' as well as occasionally turning his hand to many other sets

These are reproductions of original pen and ink drawings which are part of a George Formby set from 1940. The drawings are particularly rare for the fact that Bill Wakefield included two familiar passers-by.
© Fleetway Publications, London, 1989.

In 1937 Terry Wakefield was given his first chance to draw the characters his father represented every week. Some thumbnail sketches were required for *The Laurel & Hardy Book of Wisecracks*, a small booklet to be given away in a Booster Number of *Film Fun*. Terry completed the task overnight, submitting the 14 drawings to the editor the next morning for a fee of £7. The drawings are reproduced here in their original size.
© Fleetway Publications, London, 1989.

in *Film Fun*. Sadly, by the end of the decade Terry's art style had fallen out of fashion and he was unable to find work. After a lifetime in comics his only other skill was his ability to drive. Until his retirement in 1976 he was a driver for the West Middlesex Hospital, now and then producing cartoons for the hospital magazine.

Bill and Terry Wakefield made an important contribution to comic art. But although their work appeared in many publications it will always be uniquely identified with that of one of Britain's most popular weeklies – *Film Fun*. Never before, or since, has a comic been produced based on one particular art-style, and it remained paramount for almost 40 years.

The waiter brought the lobster and placed it before Stan Laurel and Joe E. Brown.

A sudden gust of wind blew the old gent's hat off.

The fellow was standing with one hand in his trousers pocket, and in his other hand he held a match with its head firmly pressed against the wheel.

"Looking into the scullery, I saw something which gave me an awful shock."

FILM FUN
"Would you believe it, sir! That's 'two' bad!"
"My dear old Stan!"
"My dear old Olly! Shake!"
"Of course there aren't any tigers in West Africa! I killed them all!"
FILM FUN
"The next morning I helped the crew to catch the shark."
"I picked up a long bar of soap and threw it towards the drowning man."
"His whiskers caught fire!"
FILM FUN
FILM FUN
REMOVA
"The driver got down from his seat and ran over himself."
"Do you watch the sunset often, my lad?"
"He got properly tied up and the crowd laughed heartily."

Bill Wakefield died in 1942. When his son Terry returned from serving in the Second World War, he was offered the chance to take over his father's premier set, which he immediately accepted. This superior example of his work is the front page of the 1946 Christmas Number of *Film Fun* (*right*). Note the traditional holly-bordered panels and consider how similar is Terry Wakefield's style to that of his father.
© Fleetway Publications, London, 1989.

Terry Wakefield's final set for *Film Fun* was Terry-Thomas (*below*) which he drew from 1957 to 1959 when changing styles dictated that he retire. His style of drawing and lettering here has changed somewhat, having become 'looser' over the years, but it is still instantly recognisable as vintage Wakefield. Below: a drawing specially commissioned from Terry Wakefield by the author in the late 1970s. It showed then that after 20 years of retirement his depiction of the *Film Fun* characters was as good as ever. And for once, without the threat of a deadline, he managed to add detail that ensures that it is one of his best works. The film stars around the table are those drawn both by him and his father.
© Fleetway Publications, London, 1989.

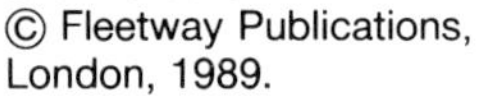

No. 1,406. Every Tuesday. December 28th, 1946.

This Week: "A CHRISTMAS WISH!"

Hallo, Folks It was pretty rough on Stan and Olly that they only had a shilling between them and the workhouse, especially as it was Christmas time. Olly was NOT overjoyed when he observed his pal Stan giving it to an old dame.

2. Yes, folks, our little lump of laughter handed the gypsy woman their shilling, and in return she presented Stan with an old vase. She informed him in ladylike and gentle tones that it would grant them any wish they made. The boys were somewhat surprised.

3. It must be mentioned that the weather was somewhat umptidoodlum, which, being translated into plain English, means that it was rather mild for the time of year. Olly thought it would be a good idea if he went to a place where there was plenty of snow and ice.

4. As soon as he rubbed the vase, it seemed that the lads were transported through the air, and then they suddenly found themselves in a cold place. It wasn't so much the iciness of the climate that put the wind up Olly, but the sight of a very big polar bear.

5. When it looked as if the bear were about to make a meal off Olly, he quickly rubbed the vase and wished he was a bit farther south—in fact, as far away as possible from the bear. The animal obviously intended to do our famous fat friend a bit of no good.

6. Again the lads were transported through the jolly old air with the greatest of ease. This time they found themselves at the South Pole, which was even c-c-colder than the last spot. There they were on an iceberg, bobbing up and down. It was cold enough to freeze the whiskers off a brass monkey. Does look awful, eh?

7. In fact, it was cold enough to freeze two lots of whiskers off two brass monkeys. Then Olly wished that he could be in a warm climate, so he rubbed the vase most vigorously and hoped for the best. Stanley had a feeling that his fat friend's wish would soon be granted. I wonder! You will see. (*Continued on back page.*)

1. Leisure is a pleasure where Frank's concerned, and he's just settling down to take it easy for the day when he sights Bill Bounce, the Ruffstuff Rovers' secretary, approaching.

2. Bounce is always on the bawl, and when he asks anyone to do him a favour he doesn't wait to hear them refuse. "Paint a poster advertising our match, Frank!" warbles he.

3. "What a sauce!" snorts our hero. "They say it pays to advertise, but Bounce won't pay for that poster. I'll show I'm not bound to do it," he adds, binding his hand.

4. "Hurt your hand, eh?" booms Bounce. "Never mind. I can still make use of you. Distribute these ten thousand hand-bills with your left hand! Thanks for your help!"

5. Frank doesn't mean to be talked into it. "What a bind!" he sniffs. "I shall have to pretend my other hand's out of action." So once again he applies some first aid, as shown.

6. He hopes this will prevent him coming off second best. But nothing gets Bounce down for long. He bobs up with another bright idea. "I can still use you," he cries.

7. "Step this way, Frank," babbles Bounce. "I know you're bent on helping advertise our footer match. Try these for size!" Saying which, he slaps a set of sandwich-boards on our pal. What a 'carry-on' for old Frank!

8. "Football advertising, indeed!" snorts Frank. "This is Bounce's job. I'll show him he can't swing it on me. For a kick-off I'll wrap things up for his benefit!" He starts off by wrapping up his jolly old left hoof.

9. "Look, I've got gout!" bleats Frank to Bounce. "Sorry I shan't be able to carry your sandwich-boards now. All I can do is hop it!" That's what HE thinks! "You can stand and control the crowd!" says Bounce.

A selection of Terry Wakefield pages from the late Forties and early Fifties. Note that two of his father's regular sets, 'George Formby' and 'Joe E. Brown', are among them.

© Fleetway Publications, London, 1989.

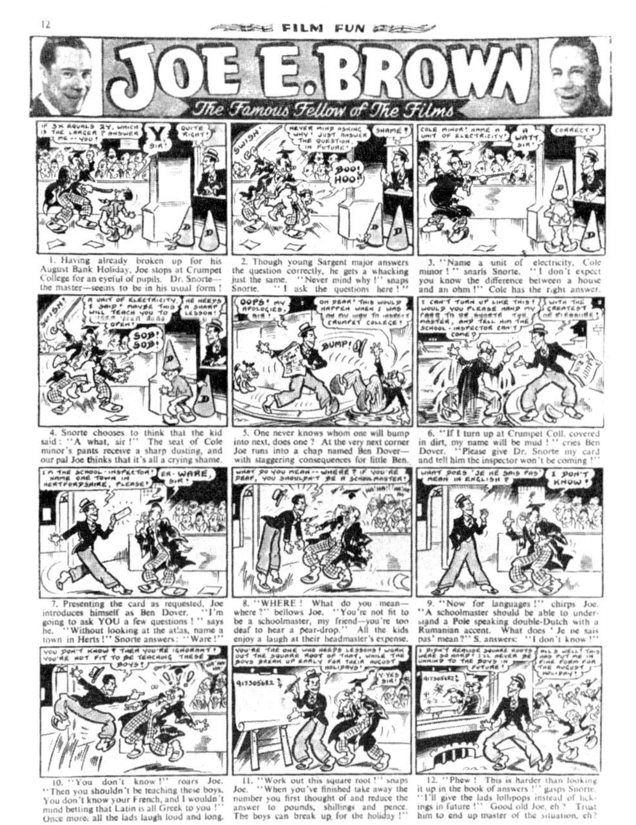

H. S. FOXWELL

Opposite
Tiger Tim had appeared on page one of *The Rainbow* from the first issue dated 14 February 1914, drawn by Julius Stafford Baker. As good as his drawings were, however, his pictures were standard fare, eight to the page, and his beasts solemn and static. Here, the improvements Foxwell brought to the feature are plain for all to see: an interesting eye-catching single drawing with the Bruin Boys bearing more than a hint of the 'jolly' look that Foxwell was to bring to them later.
© Fleetway Publications, London, 1989.

Overleaf
Foxwell used all his skills to produce the front page of this Grand Christmas Number of *The Rainbow*, dated Christmas Day, 1915.
© Fleetway Publications, London, 1989.

Page 63
Tiger Tim's Weekly (second series) as it appeared each week for 19 years with one large picture (bigger than usual as the issue is a Christmas Number) by Foxwell and an 'L' shaped accompanying set, 'The Bumpty Boys', drawn by another artist, Fred Crompton.
© Fleetway Publications, London, 1989.

Anthropomorphism has for some time existed as a sub-genre of comics and comic art. In the United States the finest examples of 'funny animal' picture strips were George Herriman's 'Krazy Kat' and Walt Kelly's 'Pogo'. The former was both zany and surreal and found favour with the nation's intellectuals; it has been hailed as the world's greatest comic strip. 'Pogo', the comic strip about a possum and the supporting cast of Okefenokee Swamp, was idiosyncratic and frequently political. Both were aimed at, and read by, adult audiences.

Britain's 'funny animal' picture strips were never so sophisticated, and were never aimed at adults. Yet some of the finest work in this genre was produced by a handful of little-known names who are only now beginning to receive the recognition they so richly deserve: Mary Tourtel who created and drew Rupert Bear of the *Daily Express*; Austin Payne, responsible for Pip, Squeak and Wilfred, the dog, penguin and rabbit trio who appeared in the pages of the *Daily Mirror*; and Herbert Foxwell whose pen and ink drawings and colour paintings of Tiger Tim and Teddy Tail, the latter of the *Daily Mail*, delighted millions between the wars.

Herbert Sydney Foxwell was born on 20 April 1890, at Camberwell, London. Shortly after, the family moved to Eltham where he grew up. Before the 1914–1918 war H. S. Foxwell spent his late teenage years studying fine art at The Addey & Stanhope College of Science, Art and Technology in Deptford. He chose art as his career and his father, Sydney Harold Foxwell, a journalist and publisher, helped him to obtain an interview at the Amalgamated Press.

In 1913 he was given his own small set, 'Artie Artichoke' which appeared in *The Favorite Comic*, followed by 'Harold Hazbean' in *Comic Cuts* in 1914. Neither of these picture strips was particularly noteworthy; he was yet to find his true metier.

Foxwell served in the Army during the First World War and held the rank of captain when the Armistice came in 1918. But throughout the war he still managed to contribute to two other comic papers: *The Rainbow* and *Puck*. No. 1 of *The Rainbow* had been issued on 14 February 1914, under the editorship of William Fisher. It was the first of what proved to be a series of 'nursery comics' published by the AP. This was a new venture in periodical publishing; earlier comics had been aimed solely at adults, but as the publishing industry expanded to serve the needs of a better-educated public, other types of reading captured adult interest. Comic publishers adjusted their sights to aim at what they saw, quite correctly, as a huge and un-

THE RAINBOW
THE IDEAL HOLIDAY PAPER FOR CHILDREN!
THE RAINBOW
SUMMER DOUBLE NUMBER
THE RAINBOW 2d.
SEASIDE STATION
LOOK! I'VE CAUGHT A WHALE.
TO BED
FOXWELL
No. 79. Vol. 2.
What jolly times those Bruin Boys are having at the seaside! Joey thinks he has caught a whale and Jacko thinks *he* has caught something, too! Look at Bobby Bruin filling Tiger Tim's "boat." What naughty boys they are! *(More of their adventures on Page 7.)*
August 14, 1915.

THE RAINBOW.
The Ideal Christmas Paper For Children.
THE RAINBOW.
CHRISTMAS DOUBLE NUMBER
THE RAINBOW
2d
A MERRY CHRISTMAS TO ALL OF US
TOYS
FOXWELL
Santa Claus did not forget to visit the Bruin Boys on Christmas Eve, and, of course, they all appeared to be fast asleep. But do you think any of them were? Just look at them! Joey doesn't look very sleepy, does he? Neither does Tiger Tim and Jacko. They found heaps and heaps of toys in their stockings, and they wish Christmas Eve were *every night!*
No. 98. Vol. 2.
December 25, 1915.

TIGER TIM'S 2d WEEKLY — THE IDEAL CHRISTMAS PRESENT FOR CHILDREN: "TIGER TIM'S ANNUAL." NOW ON SALE 6/-

TIGER TIM'S 2D WEEKLY. CHRISTMAS NUMBER.

THE BUMPTY BOYS & SANTA CLAUS. No. 110. EVERY THURSDAY. DEC. 22, 1923.

1. On Christmas Eve, the Bumpty Boys hung their stockings up. "Santa Claus won't get much into these!" said Humpty. "Let's get his sack!"

2. Then Bumpty had a fine idea. "Look, boys!" he said. "We'll put these roller-skates here, so that Santa Claus puts his feet into them and tumbles down!"

3. So they put the skates there; and then they all jumped back into bed again. "Hush! Here he comes," Bumpty cried. And down the chimney came Santa.

"We'll give those Bumpty Boys a treat!" said Tiger Tim on Christmas Eve. So off went the Bruin Boys with different instruments to play carols outside Bumpty House. And, oh dear, didn't they make a noise! Bumpty tried to throw some water over them, but luckily for them the water in the jug was frozen!

4. And his feet went right into the straps of those roller-skates! "Here he is!" Bumpty cried. "Get ready to seize his sack, boys!" But Santa Claus was saying: "Oo-oo! What has happened to my feet?"

5. And I believe that Santa Claus was quite scared! "Oh, goodness!" he cried. "I can't stop myself!" And weren't the Bumpty Boys surprised, too! "Look!" cried Humpty. "He's sliding out of the door!"

6. Away went Santa Claus past their window. "Oh, please fill our stockings, Santa Claus!" they all cried. "I'm sorry; but I can't stop now, boys!" he replied. But he came back later with some *lovely* toys.

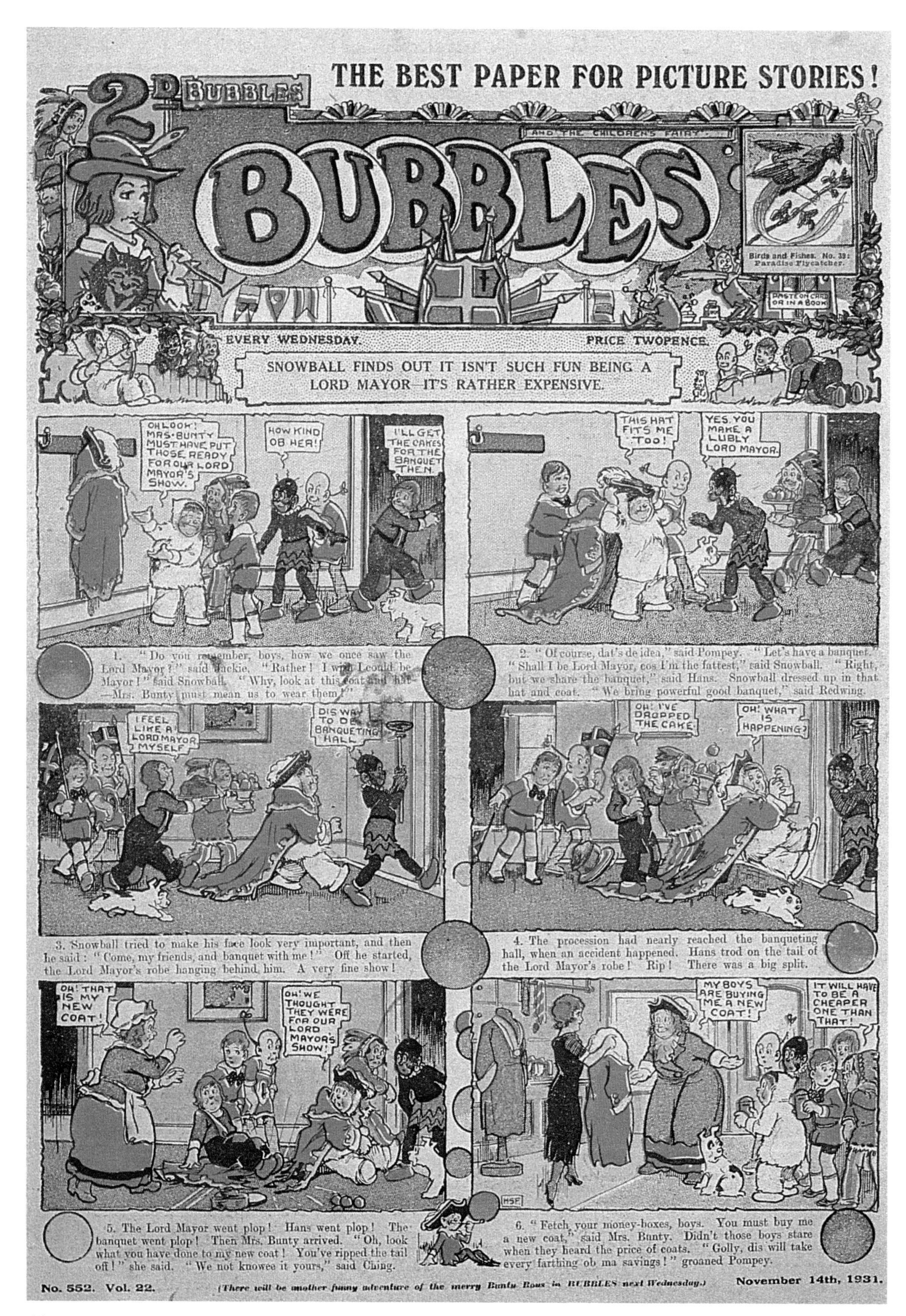
THE BEST PAPER FOR PICTURE STORIES!
2D BUBBLES
AND THE CHILDREN'S FAIRY
BUBBLES
Birds and Fishes. No. 39: Paradise Flycatcher.
PASTE ON CARD OR IN A BOOK
EVERY WEDNESDAY.
PRICE TWOPENCE.
SNOWBALL FINDS OUT IT ISN'T SUCH FUN BEING A LORD MAYOR—IT'S RATHER EXPENSIVE.
OH LOOK! MRS. BUNTY MUST HAVE PUT THOSE READY FOR OUR LORD MAYOR'S SHOW.
HOW KIND OB HER!
I'LL GET THE CAKES FOR THE BANQUET THEN.
THIS HAT FITS ME TOO!
YES. YOU MAKE A LUBLY LORD MAYOR.
1. "Do you remember, boys, how we once saw the Lord Mayor?" said Jackie. "Rather! I wish I could be Mayor!" said Snowball. "Why, look at this coat and hat —Mrs. Bunty must mean us to wear them!"
2. "Of course, dat's de idea," said Pompey. "Let's have a banquet." "Shall I be Lord Mayor, cos I'm the fattest," said Snowball. "Right, but we share the banquet," said Hans. Snowball dressed up in that hat and coat. "We bring powerful good banquet," said Redwing.
I FEEL LIKE A LORD MAYOR MYSELF
DIS WAY TO DE BANQUETING HALL
OH! I'VE DROPPED THE CAKE.
OH! WHAT IS HAPPENING?
3. Snowball tried to make his face look very important, and then he said: "Come, my friends, and banquet with me!" Off he started, the Lord Mayor's robe hanging behind him. A very fine show!
4. The procession had nearly reached the banqueting hall, when an accident happened. Hans trod on the tail of the Lord Mayor's robe! Rip! There was a big split.
OH! THAT IS MY NEW COAT!
OH! WE THOUGHT THEY WERE FOR OUR LORD MAYOR'S SHOW!
MY BOYS ARE BUYING ME A NEW COAT!
IT WILL HAVE TO BE A CHEAPER ONE THAN THAT!
HSF
5. The Lord Mayor went plop! Hans went plop! The banquet went plop! Then Mrs. Bunty arrived. "Oh, look what you have done to my new coat! You've ripped the tail off!" she said. "We not knowee it yours," said Ching.
6. "Fetch your money-boxes, boys. You must buy me a new coat," said Mrs. Bunty. Didn't those boys stare when they heard the price of coats. "Golly, dis will take every farthing ob ma savings!" groaned Pompey.
No. 552. Vol. 22.
(There will be another funny adventure of the merry Bunty Boys in BUBBLES next Wednesday.)
November 14th, 1931.

Reproductions of original drawings by Foxwell for the front page of *Bubbles*, the charming AP weekly pictured opposite. The drawings are pen and ink, the colouring and captions beneath the pictures were the responsibility of the AP staff.
© Fleetway Publications, London, 1989.

tapped youth market. The advent of *The Rainbow* was a further extension of this.

For *The Rainbow* Foxwell drew 'Sam the Skipper' and 'Dolliwog's Doll House', two pleasant, but again not particularly noteworthy, picture sets. The real star of *The Rainbow* was Tiger Tim, drawn by Julius Stafford Baker, one of the best comic artists working around and after the turn of the century. The characters of Tiger Tim and his chums, the Bruin Boys, were not new to Baker: he had first depicted them nearly ten years prior to the publication of *The Rainbow* when asked to submit a one-off three-picture comic strip to the *Daily Mirror* entitled 'Mrs Hippo's Kinder-Garten' which appeared on 16 April 1904. In November 1904 he was commissioned to draw them on a regular basis for *The Monthly Playbox*, the children's supplement to the magazine *The World and his Wife*, where they were extremely popular for many years. The supplement lasted until 1910 when the magazine was discontinued; after that Tiger Tim was transferred to a succession of magazines in which he made a regular appearance well into the 1930s. Baker also regularly drew the character for *The Playbox Annual*, the first edition

TIGER TIM'S
ANNUAL
1923
MILK
HSF

The second, third and fourth editions of *Tiger Tim's Annual* (1922–57). Note how Tim and the Bruin Boys have changed after a few years, becoming more rounded and 'fleshed out'. © Fleetway Publications, London, 1989.

of which was dated 1909. He had thus been the natural choice to depict Tim and the Bruin Boys on the front page of *The Rainbow*. After Baker, artist S. J. Cash also drew Tiger Tim for a short period.

Within a few months Foxwell was invited to take over and both the art and appearance of the set immediately began to improve. The difference was really that of style. Although an extremely good artist, Baker drew the feature as a comic strip, his manner similar to that of the great American cartoonist James Swinnerton (1875–1974), an enormously prolific and inventive artist, also known for his 'funny animal' strips, whose work appeared in the newspaper comics of William Randolph Hearst. Baker's beasts were humanised, spindly caricatures of animals. Herbert Foxwell's splendid drawings were of fully developed, well-rounded characters, instantly recognisable likenesses of animals in human form. Never perfect

The main stars of *The Playbox* were Tiger Tilly and the Hippo Girls. Foxwell drew them for eight years (1925–33). © Fleetway Publications, London, 1989.

Issued from the Offices of The Playbox, The Fleetway House, Farringdon Street, London, E.C.4.

The title page of *Mrs Hippo's Annual* 1927 showing Foxwell's variation on an Arabian theme. © Fleetway Publications, London, 1989.

The inside of the weekly *Playbox* was as delightful as the outside (*above*). *Below*, the type of six-picture set which delighted the nursery toddlers. © Fleetway Publications, London, 1989.

when depicting humans, Foxwell's art immediately came alive when he drew animals. He had found his metier.

Foxwell's drawings appeared in two other new comic titles in the next few years: *Puck* (1916) and *The Children's Fairy* (1919). It was also in 1919 that his work appeared in *Tiger Tim's Tales*, a monthly story paper for young children, the title of which was changed in 1920 to *Tiger Tim's Weekly* with renumbering from No. 1. This new nursery comic had

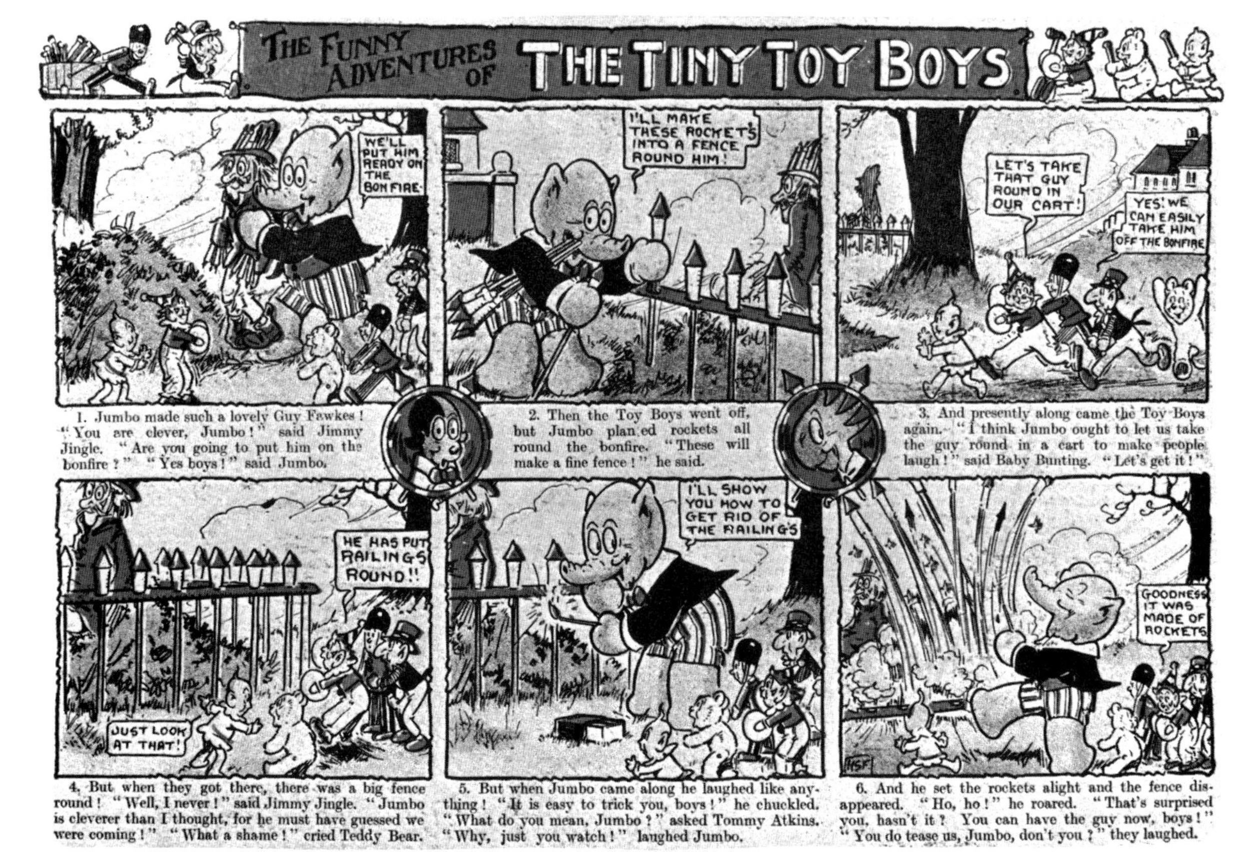

two picture strips by Foxwell, who also supplied illustrations of Tiger Tim. With the issue of 19 November 1921 the weekly was remodelled, again starting from No. 1. This second series of *Tiger Tim's Weekly* was tabloid-sized with a full-colour front page (the first series was smaller with page one printed in red and black), so that it was now in the same format as its companion comic *The Rainbow*.

In 1921 Foxwell was drawing Tiger Tim for three different publications: *Tiger Tim's Weekly*, where Tim and his chums were pictured in one 80 mm × 15 mm panel which occupied nearly half the front page and with additional interior illustrations which accompanied the text; *The Rainbow*, where the Bruin Boys had the entire front page with a six-picture set in full colour; and *The Playbox Annual*, for which he contributed beautiful colour plates and pen and ink drawings.

Always excellent, Herbert Foxwell's art was sometimes breathtaking, notably on special occasions when he was asked for a front page for a Christmas, Summer or Easter Number. He would convert this into one big picture, experimenting with style and design in a manner that was then quite new to comics. Foxwell was obviously proud of his work: as early as 1915 he was signing his drawings with either a bold 'Foxwell' or his initials 'HSF'. The fact that AP allowed him to do so is a measure of the regard in which he was held. Few other artists, if any, signed their work at this time.

The 1920s were the golden age of Foxwell art. In 1921 AP issued yet another nursery comic, *Bubbles*, which again gave pride of place to Foxwell's drawings. For this he drew 'Mr Croc's School' and 'Mrs Bunty's Boarding School', which were printed in colour on the front page. And in 1925 AP revived the old title of *The Playbox*, turning it into a weekly nursery comic for girls. The front page stars in this instance were not the Bruin Boys but the Hippo Girls, carbon copies, with the sex changed, of Tim and his chums. Besides 'Mrs Hippo's Boarding School' Foxwell also found time to produce work for the inside pages. By 1927 his work was appearing in no less than four weekly comics and six annuals, always on page one of the weeklies and on the covers of the annuals, the latter being reproduced from his water-colour paintings. Foxwell's talent for drawing comic animals was such that rather like Bill Wakefield and his drawings of celebrities, he was in a

In 1933 Herbert Foxwell left the Amalgamated Press to work for Associated Newspapers, owners of *The Daily Mail* and *Sunday Dispatch*. To the latter he contributed 'The Adventures of Jolly Jack' and other work for the junior section of the newspaper, a part of a front page of which is shown here.
© Fleetway Publications, London, 1989.

Opposite
The Hippo Girls were popular enough for the publisher to give them their own annual (1926–40). The cover of this 1928 edition is from a watercolour painting by Foxwell.
© Fleetway Publications, London, 1989.

Another nursery weekly which featured Foxwell's work was *The Playbox*, where the front page stars were 'The Chummy Boys'. Again, Foxwell uses his favourite design of large picture with cheerful surround. Note the advertisement at bottom right for the 1932 *Playbox Annual* priced at six shillings, very expensive at the time.
© Fleetway Publications, London, 1989.

class of his own.

Great consternation must have ensued when in 1933 Foxwell announced that he was thereafter going to be working exclusively for the *Daily Mail* on its children's picture feature 'Teddy Tail'. The crisis was overcome – doubtless with some difficulties – by calling upon the services of long-time staff member Bert Wymer who soon proved himself a worthy successor.

The paper shortages of the Second World War put paid to many comics and annuals: *Tiger Tim's Weekly* was discontinued in May 1940 and the weekly *Bubbles* in 1941. *Rainbow*, *Playbox* and their accompanying annuals, together with *Tiger Tim's Annual*, were in print until the mid-1950s. However, none of the artwork was ever as ebullient as that of Foxwell.

'Teddy Tail' had first appeared in the *Daily Mail* in 1915, drawn by the artist Charles Folkard who soon left the strip to concentrate on book illustration. He was replaced by his brother, Harry, who was the regular artist until the 1930s. On 8 April 1933 the *Daily Mail* decided to publish a weekly comic supplement, *The Boy's and Girl's Daily Mail*. The first choice for a front page comic character was naturally Teddy Tail and the artist Harry Folkard.

The idea of rejuvenating the famous mouse by asking Herbert Foxwell to take him on came from Stanley Bell, editor-in-chief of *The Daily Mail*, who was an admirer of Foxwell's *Tiger Tim* work. Foxwell's first Teddy Tail page was published on 4 November 1933 and he continued to draw the feature (sometimes for two editions a week) and other strips for the inside pages for the next two years until the circulation war had moved on to another front and the supplement was discontinued. The *Teddy Tail Annual*, first issued for 1934 and for each subsequent year up to the 1941 edition, had covers and

MRS HIPPO'S
ANNUAL
1928
FOXWELL

THE PLAYBOX 2D
THE JOLLIEST CHRISTMAS PRESENT
"PLAYBOX ANNUAL"
NOW ON SALE
6/-
THE PLAYBOX 2D
CHRISTMAS NUMBER
No. 358. Vol. 9. EVERY FRIDAY. December 26th, 1931
A HAPPY CHRISTMAS TO ALL OF US
THAT'S BROUGHT ALL THOSE CRACKERS DOWN!
DAT WAS HARD TO PULL
PLAYBOX
JOLLY CHRISTMAS FUN!
Oh, what a jolly time the Chummy Boys had on Christmas Day! "Ha, ha! We are going to raid the Christmas tree!" chuckled Bronko. "Take your choice, Andy!" But when Mrs. Chummy came in she soon put a stop to their tricks! Ha, ha!

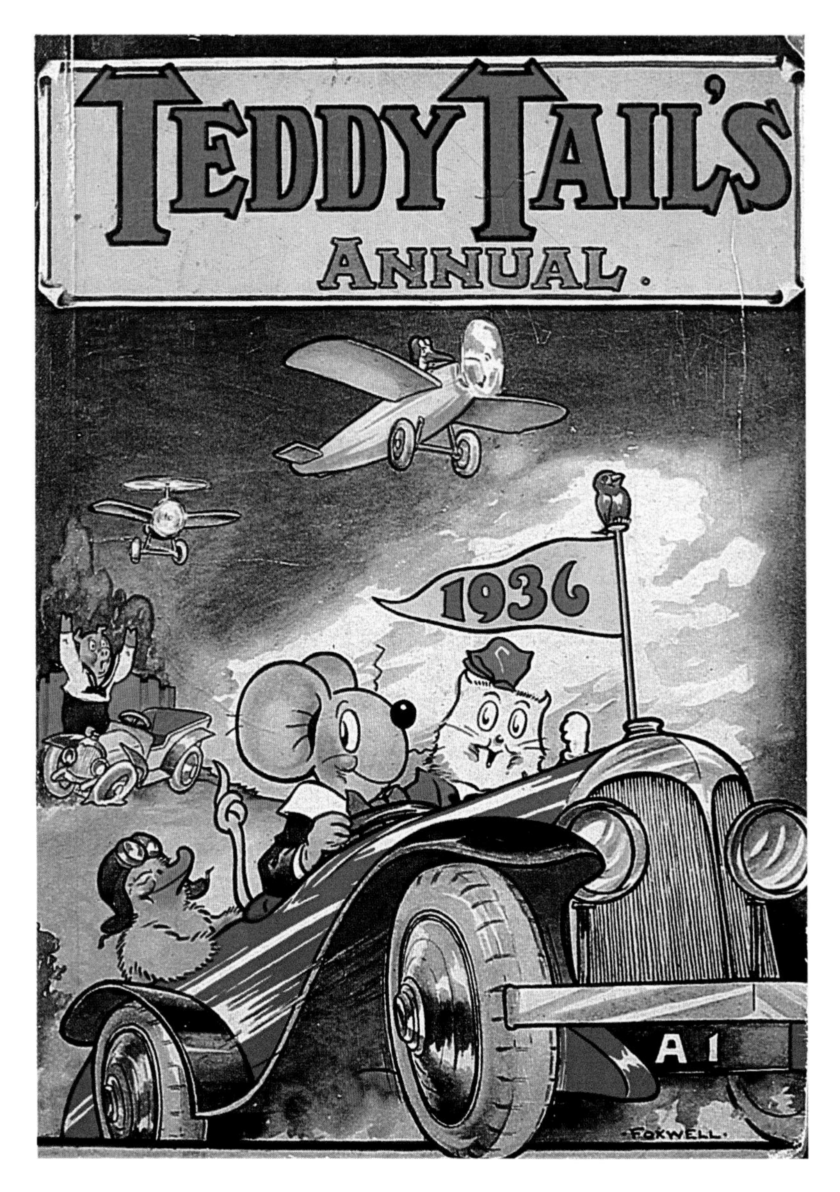

Besides the paintings and drawings he did each year for *Teddy Tail's Annual*, Foxwell also helped to produce merchandising material such as jigsaw puzzles, bookends and other books. He also supplied the pictures used on birthday cards that were sent to members of the Teddy Tail League, a club for Teddy Tail readers. Pictured above are two of these cards.

Left
The 1936 (the third) *Teddy Tail Annual*.

The title page of the 1935 edition of *Jolly Jack's Annual*.
© Fleetway Publications, London, 1989.

interior art by Foxwell for all but the last volume. He also painted a series of birthday cards for the Teddy Tail League, a club for followers of the famous mouse.

Another newspaper published by Associated Newspapers, who owned the *Daily Mail*, was the *Sunday Dispatch*, which also decided to issue a free comic. The first was included with the newspaper on 20 August 1933, and was entitled *Jolly Jack's Weekly*. Unfortunately it caught Foxwell on his weak point: Jolly Jack was an all too human character, never in the same league as Foxwell's animals. The comic was discontinued after 70 issues in December 1934.

Foxwell's personal life was not always as happy as the mood of his work. His first wife, Emily, died in 1924 of consumption and he was left with five children to bring up on his own. His sense of loss and personal hardship at this time can only be imagined, but it is a tribute to his dedication that despite all this, and a heavy workload which would often have him working through the night, there was not the slighted variance in the quality of his work. He remarried in 1934 and had another son.

The Daily Mail began to publish a weekly comic supplement on 8 April 1933. Foxwell's art appeared from 4 November of that year. Always charming, his best work was for the celebratory issues produced for Christmas and New Year. Here is a splendid example as Britain's most famous mouse and his pals ring in 1935. © Fleetway Publications, London, 1989.

After the declaration of war in September 1939, Foxwell was recalled, having been for many years in the Army Reserve. He was posted to Aldershot where he died, of natural causes, in late 1943. Old staff members of Fleetway House say that they can remember him coming to visit his previous colleagues, a tall, dark, good-looking man who appeared extremely dashing in his uniform. They also remember him for what he was: one of Britain's finest comic artists whose talent for drawing comic animals was unsurpassable.

ALLAN MORLEY

Allan Morley was born in Scarborough on 29 April 1895, the only child of a local publican, Samuel Morley, and his wife Helen. Morley senior died in 1899 when Allan was four years old, leaving Helen with the responsibility of raising their young son alone.

Allan attended school in Scarborough where he developed an early interest in art which was given a boost when he won a drawing competition at the age of 13. In 1910 Helen Morley and her young son moved south to live with an uncle in Southend. Seizing on his talent, she sent him to art school in Hendon, North London, where he studied under Tom Downey. Downey had been a pupil of the well-known Victorian caricaturist and illustrator, Alfred Bryan, and had since established himself as a leading painter, illustrator and caricaturist contributing work to numerous magazines in the 1890s.

Downey helped to develop Morley's style and encouraged him to submit drawings to the various weekly comics issued at the time by publishers James Henderson and the Amalgamated Press. Initially, these were single picture jokes. Morley's first published drawing came around 1913, probably for *The Big Comic* (Henderson). Other acceptances soon followed for both Henderson publications and those of the AP. By 1915 his work also was appearing in *Pictures & Picturegoer*, a magazine for aficionados of the cinema, for which he drew 'Our Cinematographic Cartoons'.

At the outbreak of the First World War, Morley had turned 18 and joined the army, where much of his time was spent entertaining the troops: he was a self-taught ventriloquist, who had his own small troop of dummies which he used in a stage act. In his spare time he continued to contribute cartoons to the comic papers. However, life was not without its dangers: in one incident Morley was almost killed when a Zeppelin appeared in the Essex sky and began dropping bombs. He later wrote about the event: 'I had a very narrow escape, as a bomb fell within six yards of where I stood. I saw the Zeppelin quite distinctly, and also the other two bombs fall beside the one that dropped so close to me. If it had been an explosive bomb it would have been all up with me, but luckily it was an incendiary one. We are always expecting them at night now, and hardly ever sleep until morning.' But he managed to get a good cartoon out of the incident: it depicted him looking over his shoulder at a bursting bomb, which had a label attached to it bearing the words 'A present from Willie.'

After the armistice Morley decided to make drawing his full-time occupation and was once again having his work published in both Henderson and AP comics. By this time he had

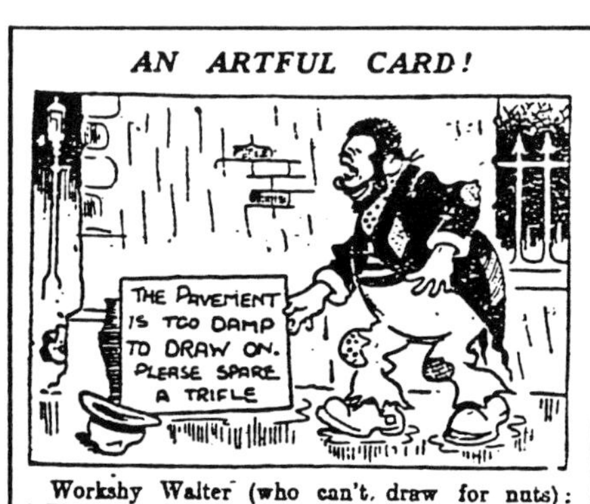

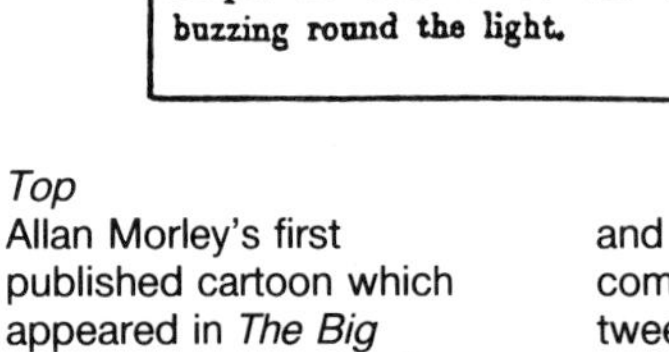

Top
Allan Morley's first published cartoon which appeared in *The Big Comic*, a James Henderson publication, around 1913. The other jokes are from different Henderson and Amalgamated Press comics published between 1915 and 1920.
© Fleetway Publications, London, 1989.

Opposite
'Homeless Hector', which appeared in *Illustrated Chips*, had been Bertie Brown's first original set in 1908. Morley took it over for a short time some years later.
© Fleetway Publications, London, 1989.

graduated from one-off jokes to small picture sets and his drawings began to achieve a certain sophistication. Popular sets of the time by Morley were 'Harry Tate' (*Merry & Bright*: 1919); 'Gilbert the Goalie' (*Funny Wonder*: 1921); 'Romo the Guide' (*Funny Wonder*: 1924) and 'Davy Deen' (*Jester*: 1925). It was also in the 1920s that he replaced artist Bertie Brown (see pp. 00) on two classic sets of the genre: 'Homeless Hector' (*Illustrated Chips*) and 'Moonlight Moggie' (*Jester*).

After the war, Allan and his mother had returned to Yorkshire, where they lived in the market town of Malton. Here he met his wife-to-be, Ethel Wray. Allan had attended a concert party where Ethel was playing

the piano. She was young (16), pretty and talented; it was love at first sight and they were married in October 1924. They had one daughter, Mary, born in 1927. Two years after his marriage, Morley and his family moved from Malton back to Scarborough, where he lived until 1948.

In 1925 Morley submitted work to R. D. Low, the editor of the *Rover*, which was published by D. C. Thomson in Dundee. The *Rover*, a new story paper which had begun publication on 4 March 1922, was the second of Thomson's 'Big Five' (*Adventure*, *Rover*, *Wizard*, *Skipper*, *Hotspur*). Low had included small picture strips from the beginning; however, most were crudely drawn and served merely as light relief from the pages of closely printed text. It must have been immediately obvious

1. Our hungry hound saw a most interesting announcement pasted on a wall t'other day. "Buckshee bones for bow-wows," it read, or words to that effect. Anyway—

2. It fairly made our prize pup's mouth water. "I'll go and fetch all my pals to see it!" wuffled he. And off he trotted to spread the gladsome news.

3. But, alas! that poster was in three sections, and when Hector returned with his college chums the billposter had completed the job, and the notice had undergone a change.

4. Poor old Hector got severely told off by those angry bow-wows, who disliked practical jokes

Harry Tate, the famous comedian of the music halls, was happy to lend his name to this four-picture set which appeared in *Merry & Bright* in 1919.
© Fleetway Publications, London, 1989.

Allan Morley's style had made obvious improvements by the time he started to draw this set for *The Funny Wonder* in 1921. He had learned how to 'animate' his drawings and made 'Gilbert' a truly comic character.
© Fleetway Publications, London, 1989.

to Low that Morley's tidy, unpretentious drawing style was perfect for the *Rover*. His first published sets were 'Willie Wiggles the Perky Postman', 'Nosey Parker Our Prize Busybody', 'Chinn & Wagg' and 'Our Artist At Work'.

For the next two years Morley drew for both D. C. Thomson and the Amalgamated Press (the comics of James Henderson had been taken over by AP in 1920). He drew single picture jokes as well as 'Homeless Hector' and, most importantly, became for a time the principal artist of 'Casey Court' (*Chips*). This large one-panel feature was beautifully drawn in the style of the feature's originator, Julius Stafford Baker, whose work Morley admired a great deal. In common with almost all the other work he did for AP, they were signed with both of his initials (his single picture jokes were usually signed with a simple 'M').

In 1927, as D. C. Thomson began to supply him with more work, he reached a 'gentleman's agreement' with the firm which meant that for the rest of his working life he would draw for Thomson exclusively. As a result, no more work was

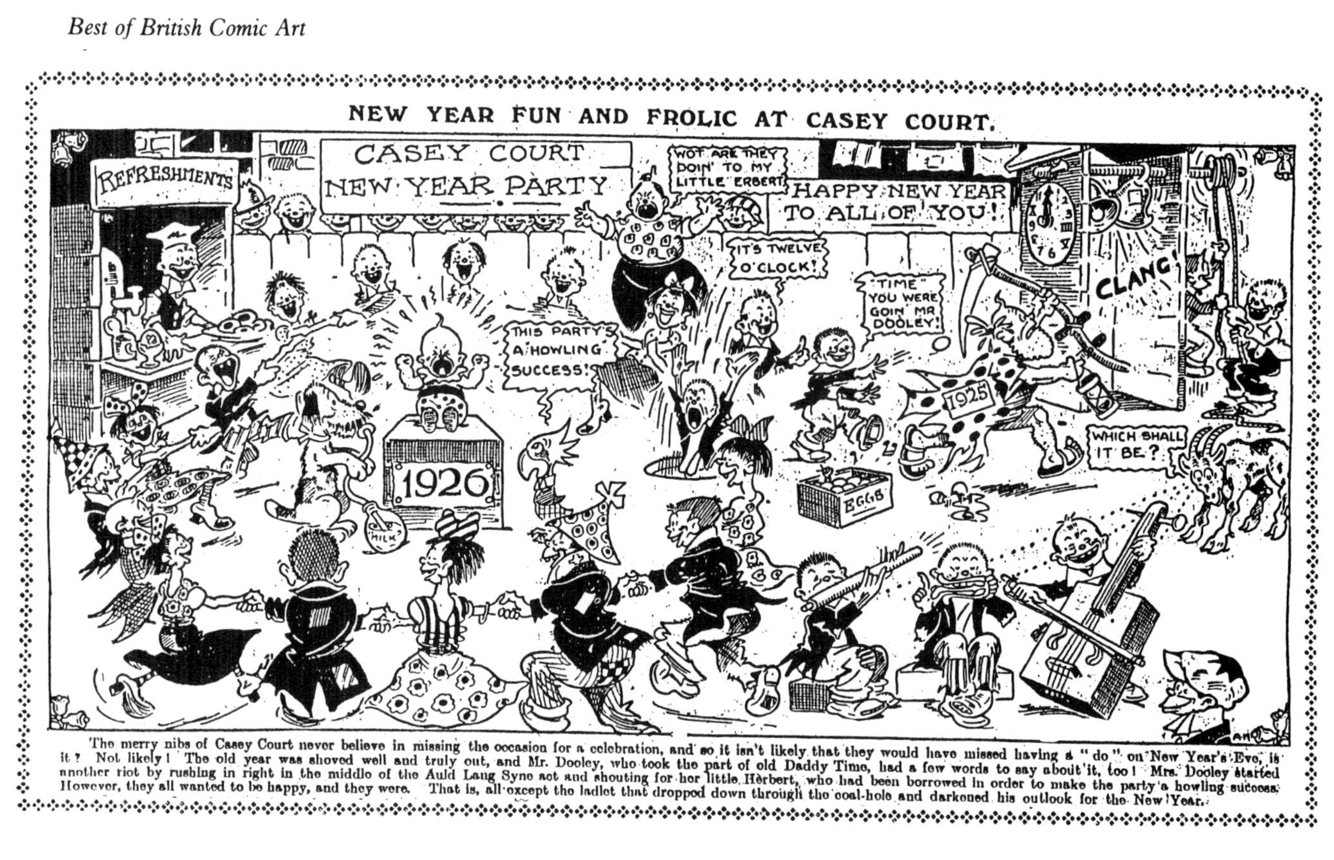

THE CASEY COURT FURNITURE STORE.

CASEY COURT FURNITURE STORES
ALL GOODS MADE IN OUR OWN FACKTRY
MANAGER W BAGGS
INSTALMINTS TAKEN
ENTRANS
FOLDING BED
PLANT STAND
SIDE BORO
CUCKOO! CUCKOO!
LARGE KOOKOO KLOCK
BETTER VERY SPRINGY
SOAP
PIANO NICE TONE
ARTERNOON TEA TABLE
NOSE BAG
FINE BILLYARD TABLE COMPLETE

Billy Baggs, the brainy young citizen of Casey Court, once had a great notion for making a little easy money. He opened an antique furniture stores. Some of the stuff dated back to the time that soap boxes were invented. His customers were not of the best, and many wanted to know too much about the stuff, with the result that some of it got badly knocked about. F'rinstance, one nosy client got boxed up in the folding bed, while another was let through the expanding dining-table. So, if there were no sales, there was plenty of excitement.

Top
'Casey Court' had first appeared in *Illustrated Chips* in 1902, drawn by Julius Stafford Baker, whom Morley greatly admired. He was therefore particularly pleased to be asked to take over the feature in 1925 (although Baker had since ceased to be the artist). Here, in the one-picture format constant for 51 years, Billy Bagg and his 'Casey Court' citizens celebrate the 1926 New Year.
© Fleetway Publications, London, 1989.

Bottom
Each week the inventive citizens of 'Casey Court' had a different theme. This week, their own furniture store. . . .
© Fleetway Publications, London, 1989.

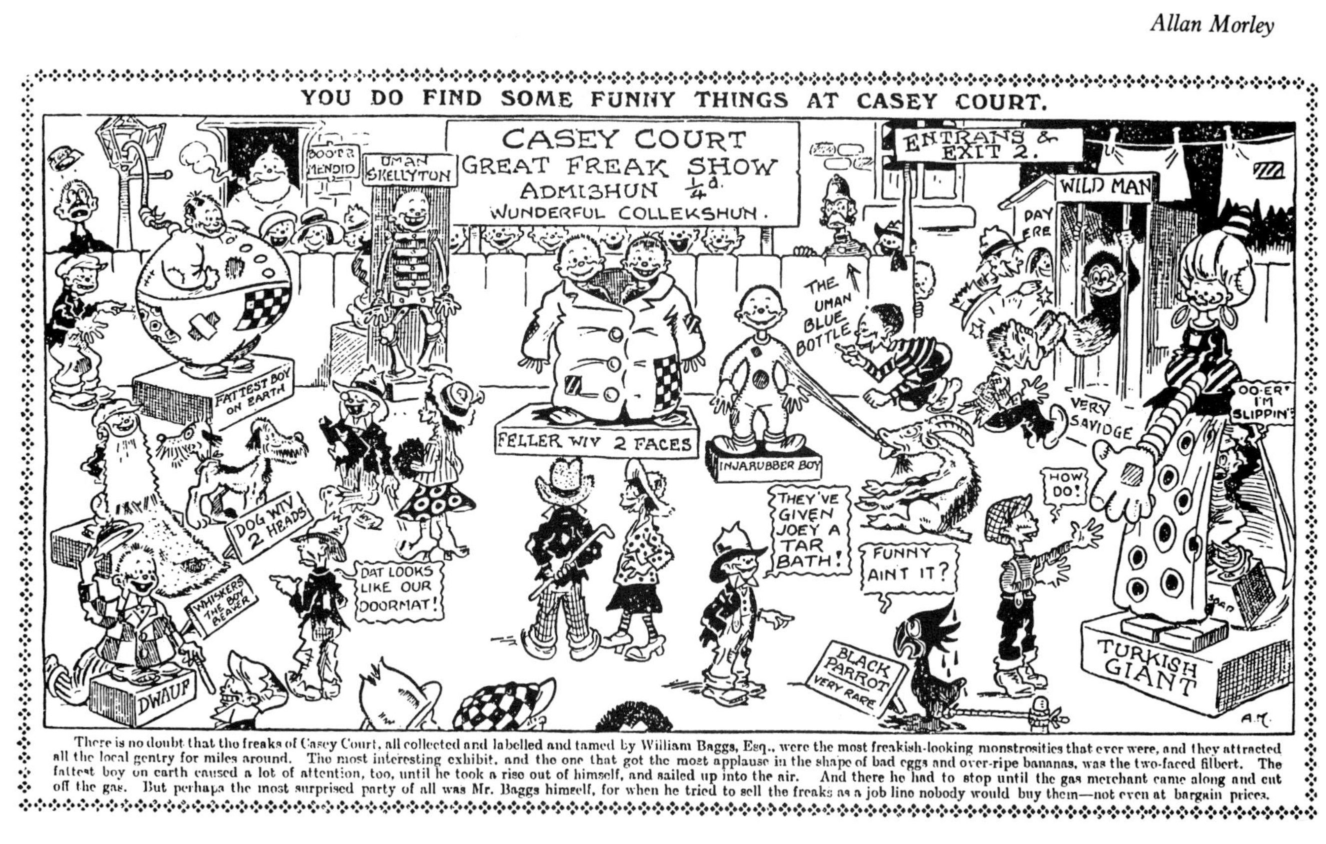

It was 'the freaks of Casey Court' when they decided to produce their own 'Great Freak Show'. . . . © Fleetway Publications, London, 1989.

submitted to AP. In the late 1920s some of his Thomson picture strips were 'Dogged Dan the Schoolboard Man' (*Adventure*: 1927), 'Scrimpy Bill' (*Rover*: 1927), and 'Roving Rufus' (*Wizard*: 1928). Many more were to follow, and he was invited to begin to initial his work for D. C. Thomson in January 1947.

During the 1930s, Allan Morley's work appeared in all of the 'Big Five' story papers. They were neat, often ingenious, little sets. Although comprising up to a dozen pictures, Thomson kept the reproduction of each to a half-page, which perfectly suited Morley's art.

On 8 March 1936, Thomson decided to include a free comic with its weekly newspaper the *Sunday Post*. It was the first comic to be published by the Scottish firm and several of Allan Morley's sets were selected for reprinting, notably: 'Nero and Zero Our Rollicking Romans (*Wizard*: 1930), 'Wishbone Wuzzy' (*Skipper*: 1934) and 'Silas Snatcher, the Truant Catcher' (*Hotspur*: 1933). These and other Morley sets were reprinted in the *Sunday Post Fun Section* for decades.

Allan Morley's best-known characters and eponymous comic strips were introduced in the first issue of Thomson's new *The Dandy Comic*, published on 4 December 1937: Keyhole Kate, Hungry Horace and Freddy the Fearless Fly. A psychiatrist could have spent many interesting months with Kate and Horace, she with a mania for inquisitiveness (like another Morley character, Nosey Parker) compulsively peering through keyholes, and Horace, the glutton, with his insatiable appetite for food. Freddy the Fly was the ultimate underdog battling (fearlessly, of course), against all the odds life could set against him. There couldn't have been three more simply constructed comic strips and no one could have guessed at their conception that they would be particularly memorable. Yet they were. Anyone of middle-age asked to recall some comic characters from *The Dandy* of their youth will very probably start by mentioning one, two or all three of these sets drawn by Allan Morley.

A companion to the successful *Dandy* was *The Beano Comic* launched on 30 July 1938, and here Morley was given his own full-page set for the first time. It could be said that he needed it: the character was 'Big Fat

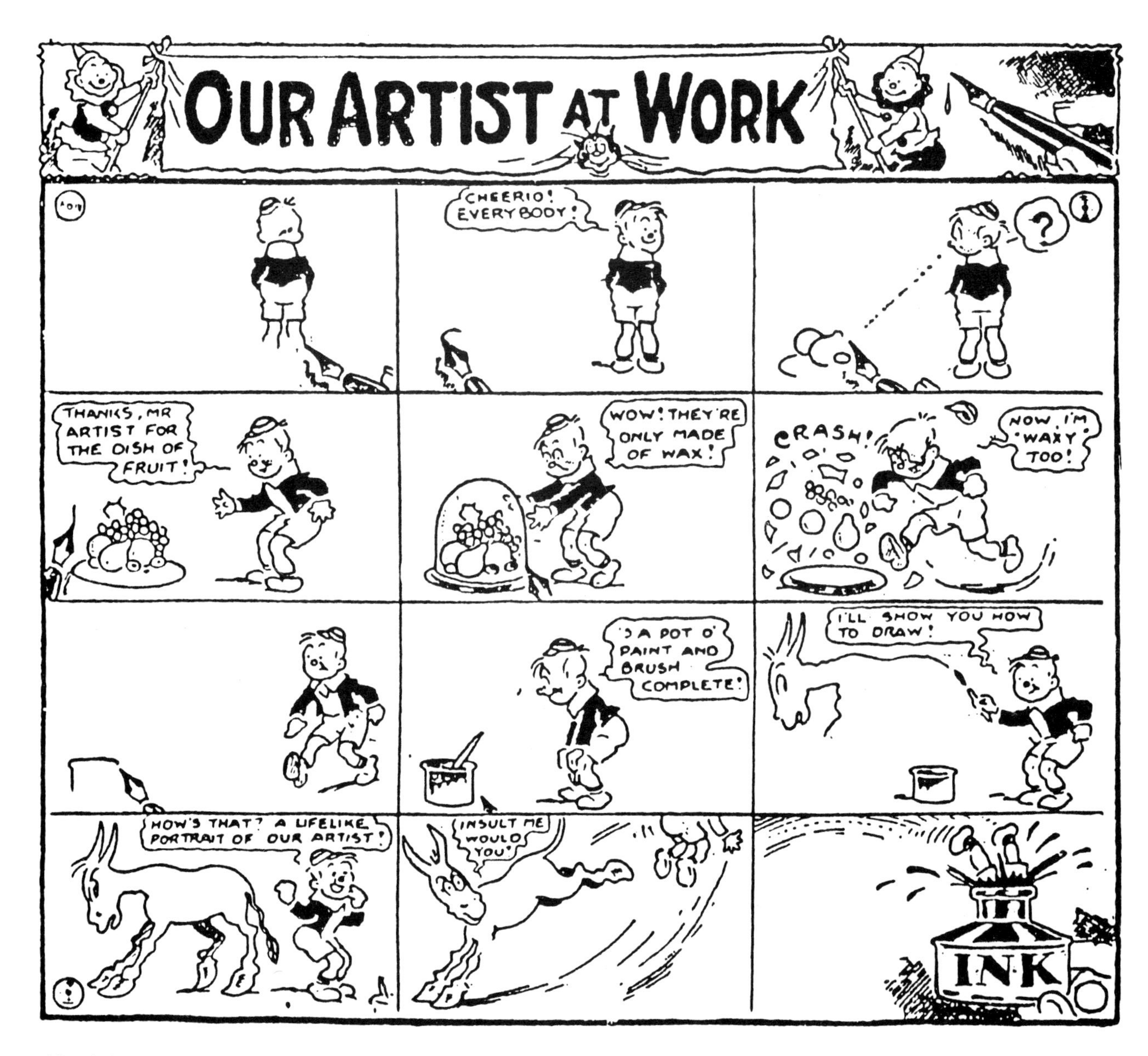

'Our Artist At Work' was one of Allan Morley's first sets for D. C. Thomson. The example shown above is c. 1925. The neat idea of the artist's drawings coming to life is reminiscent of the famous 'Out of the Inkwell' animated shorts once produced by the American Max Fleischer film studios. 'Our Artist' immediately gave Morley the opportunity to rid himself of the cluttered backgrounds so apparent in his Henderson and AP work. Morley retained the basic simplicity of his early work for D. C. Thomson all his working life. © D.C. Thomson & Co. Ltd.

Joe' ('One Ton of Fun – He Hasn't Been Weighed Since the Age of Three – the Weighing-Machine Always Broke You See!'). Morley drew the strip beautifully in eight large panels. But 'Big Fat Joe' was relatively short-lived, possibly owing to Morley's increasingly busy schedule; the character was soon incorporated into the Lord Snooty feature drawn by Dudley Watkins. Morley drew a score or more different comic sets for *The Dandy* and *The Beano* during the next 15 years; he also contributed other work to Thomson's short-lived *Magic* comic published in the late 1930s.

During the Second World War Allan Morley was too old to enlist but he did perform 'fire-watch' duty for the town. This, together with his constant sketching (he would walk around the town with his notebook jotting down ideas for comic strips), made him a well-known local figure.

The characters for his sets (Keyhole Kate, Freddie the Fearless Fly, etc.) were originated by the staff at the D. C. Thomson editorial offices, but thereafter Morley was left to his own devices. The scripts, pencils and inks were all done by him and were executed without even a 'rough' for approval by the editors. He earned a reputation as a reliable artist who could be trusted to reproduce excellent work on time.

On 7 February 1953, D. C. Thomson launched its first post-war comic: *The Topper*. Morley was still allocated only a half-page, but this time with a

'Nosey Parker' (subtitled 'Our Prize Busybody') was published in *The Rover*, *The Sunday Post Fun Section* and *The Beezer*. Morley resisted the obvious by not drawing the character with an exaggeratedly long nose, instead depicting him with an over-large head. The above is page one of a give-away comic presented with *The Rover* on 2 July 1938. © D.C. Thomson & Co. Ltd.

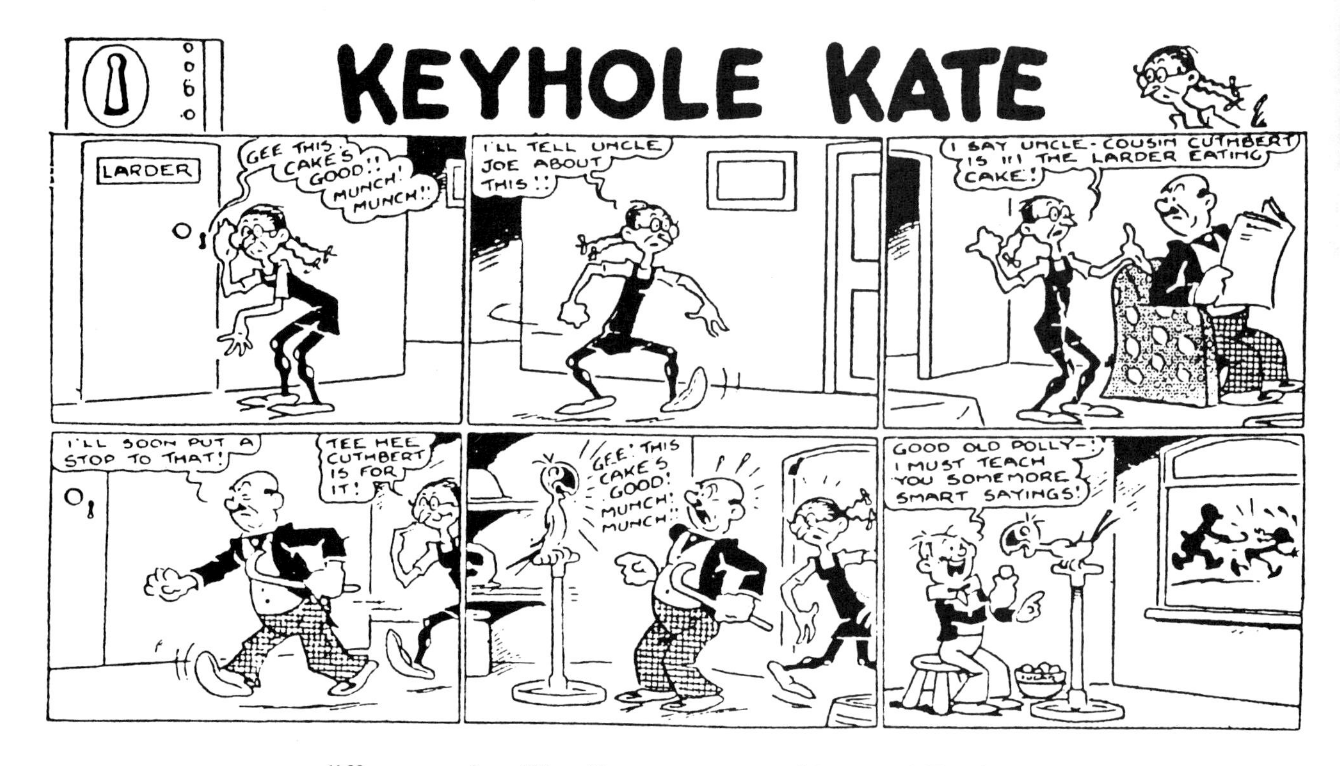

difference, for *The Topper* was a tabloid. Thus his 'Uncle Dan the Menagerie Man' had what appeared to be huge pictures in comparison with his previous work.

The Topper was successful enough to beget a companion, *The Beezer*, the first issue of which was published on 21 January 1956. For this, Thomson asked Morley to resurrect two of his earlier characters: 'Nosey Parker' and 'Nero and Zero'.

In 1948, Allan Morley and his family had moved to Greenford in Middlesex, where he lived until 1959. One reason for the move was to be nearer to London. Morley loved the capital and the south, finding it both stimulating and enjoyable, although he always retained a deep affection for the quiet seaside town of Scarborough.

Opposite and below
Allan Morley's work was a major feature of D. C. Thomson's *The Dandy Comic* when it was launched on 4 December 1937. All three of these six-picture sets became nationally famous.
© D.C. Thomson & Co. Ltd.

Circle
Allan Morley's initial drawing of 'Freddy the Fearless Fly'. Compare this with the published version above. © D.C. Thomson & Co. Ltd.

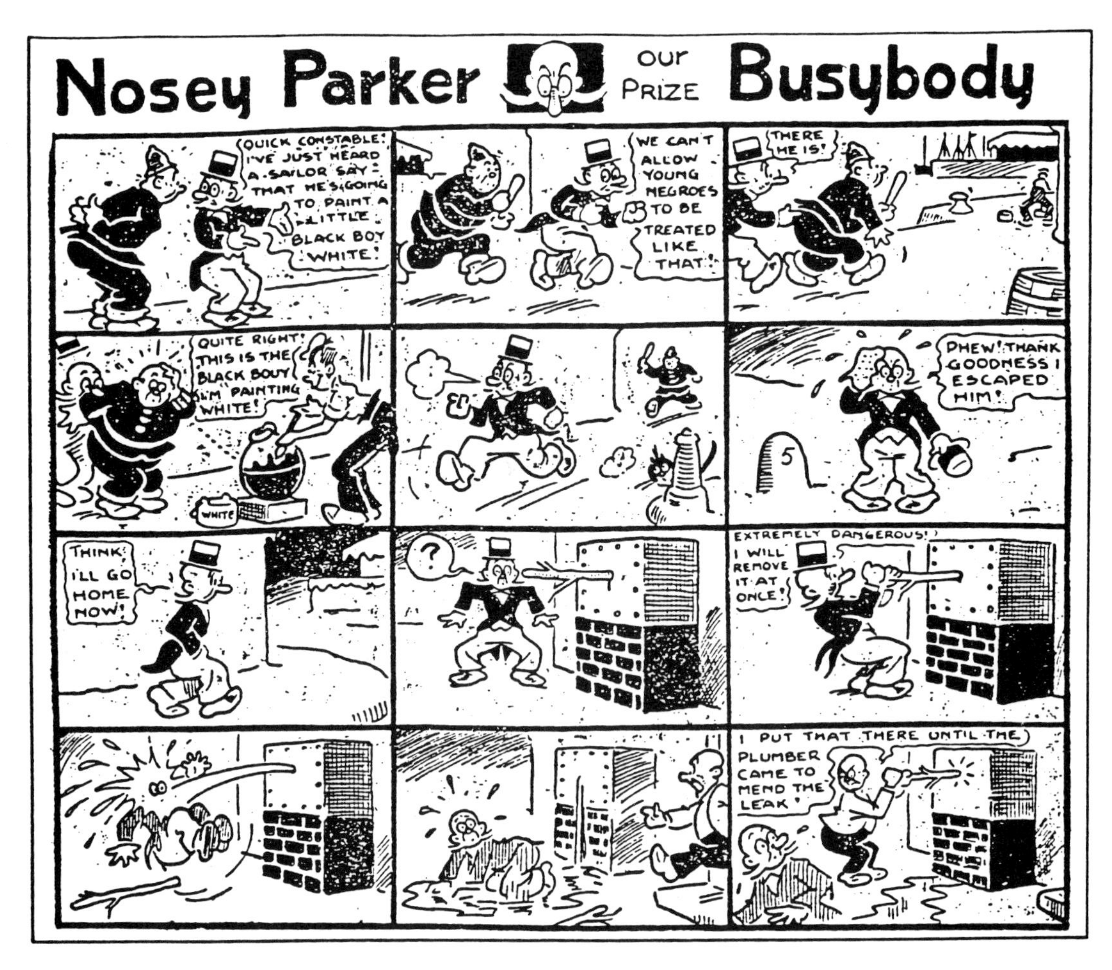

Nosey Parker OUR PRIZE Busybody
QUICK CONSTABLE! I'VE JUST HEARD A SAILOR SAY THAT HE'S GOING TO PAINT A LITTLE BLACK BOY WHITE!
WE CAN'T ALLOW YOUNG NEGROES TO BE TREATED LIKE THAT!
THERE HE IS!
QUITE RIGHT! THIS IS THE BLACK BOUY I'M PAINTING WHITE!
WHITE
PHEW! THANK GOODNESS I ESCAPED HIM!
5
THINK I'LL GO HOME NOW!
?
EXTREMELY DANGEROUS! I WILL REMOVE IT AT ONCE!
I PUT THAT THERE UNTIL THE PLUMBER CAME TO MEND THE LEAK!

NOSEY PARKER OUR PRIZE BUSY-BODY
GIVE IT TO ME AT ONCE!
NOW BE OFF WITH YOU!
I WONDER IF IT IS LOADED?
NO!
I FOUND A SMALL BOY PLAYING WITH IT!
IS IT LOADED?
NO! IT'S QUITE EMPTY. LOOK FOR YOURSELF!
PLAY JOKES ON THE FORCE EH?
COSH
TA TA! NOSEY! I HOPE YOU ENJOY YOUR SKILLY!

Left
Charlie Chutney, one of Morley's regular characters from *The Dandy* as it appeared during the Fifties.
© D. C. Thomson & Co. Ltd.

In 1959 a heart complaint, from which he had suffered for some years, became considerably worse. His doctor ordered him to avoid strenuous activity: even climbing stairs was inadvisable. So he moved to a bungalow at Cliftonville on the Kent coast. A year later, on September 1960, while the doctor was visiting him, he collapsed and died. He was aged 65.

Allan Morley made the small picture strip his forte. His style, neat and simple, was deceptive: in the manner of all true professionals, he made the difficult look easy. To produce several funny picture strips every week for 40 years was an extraordinary achievement. Morley accomplished it with the apparent ease with which he executed all his small masterpieces.

Opposite
'Nosey Parker, Our Prize Busybody', began his inquisitive career on the back page of the boys' story paper *The Rover* in 1925. Morley was still drawing the little man with a big head and a large proboscis three decades later for *The Beezer* in 1956.
© D.C. Thomson & Co. Ltd.

Old Ma Murphy, one of Morley's creations from *The Dandy* as it appeared during the Fifties.
© D.C. Thomson & Co. Ltd.

Opposite
Following the immediate success of *The Dandy Comic*, its Scottish publisher launched *The Beano Comic* on 30 July 1938. Allan Morley's contribution, 'Big Fat Joe', was later incorporated into Dudley Watkins's 'Lord Snooty'.
© D.C. Thomson & Co. Ltd.

He Hasn't Been Weighed Since the Age of Three
—The Weighing-Machine Always Broke, You See.

BIG FAT JOE

1 TON OF FUN

Above
'Nero and Zero' were also known as 'The Rollicking Romans' when they appeared in the centre pages of *The Wizard* during the Thirties. They were resurrected for D. C. Thomson's tabloid weekly *The Beezer* in 1956. © D.C. Thomson & Co. Ltd.

Below
Morley's 'Uncle Dan the Menagerie Man' was a new creation by D. C. Thomson for *The Topper*, launched in 1953. This page appeared in the 1957 *Topper Annual*. © D.C. Thomson & Co. Ltd.

SHAGGY DOGGY

THOUGH Shaggy thinks a walk's a treat,
A-chasing cats from street to street,
Alas! He won't be going today—
At home his master has to stay.

But soon young Shaggy's glad again,
For who comes in but Uncle Ben.
And though he's oh, so very ol',
He says he'll take our dog a stroll.

Now Shaggy's happy, Shaggy's gay,
And Shaggy wants to jump and play.
Old Uncle Ben knows what to do—
" The park is just the place for you!"

But now poor Shaggy sadly sighs,
For up against the wall there lies
A notice big, for all to read—
" No dogs allowed unless on lead."

But Shaggy gives a joyful bark
And soon they'll both be in the park,
For now he's got a notion bright—
He'll use Ben's beard so long and white!

The keeper's there and gets a shock,
When Ben and Shaggy take their walk.
For Shaggy's fashioned with his paws
The strangest LEASH that ever was!

Shaggy Doggy, a Fifties favourite from *The Dandy*. © D. C. Thomson & Co. Ltd.

Julius Sneezer 'the Sneezing Caesar' with the remarkable nose. Morley's 1950's version of ancient Rome. © D. C. Thomson & Co. Ltd.

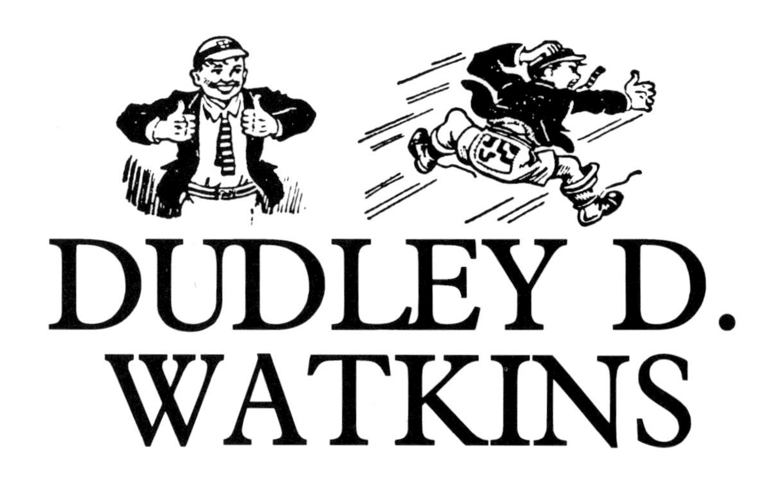

DUDLEY D. WATKINS

For more than 30 years Dudley Dexter Watkins was the best-known comic artist in Britain. There were two reasons for this: firstly, Watkins was a master craftsman, a penman of remarkable ability who was equally at home with either the comic or adventure strip; and secondly, he was allowed to sign his work, which brought his name to the attention of millions. Nearly all of his drawings and paintings appeared in the publications of D. C. Thomson, the Scottish publisher with offices in Dundee. It is for this reason that many have assumed – wrongly – that Watkins also originated from north of the border. In fact he was born in Manchester on 27 February 1907, and raised in Nottingham, the eldest of three children.

Dudley Watkins's father was a lithographic artist and his son was quick to display his inherited artistic skill: when he was six, Dudley received a commendation from Nottingham's mayor for his drawing of a parade, and by the time he was eleven, his work was on display at an exhibition held at Nottingham Castle, with four pictures he had painted of the city's historical pageant. In 1919, he attended evening classes at Nottingham School of Art and, in the early 1920s, he took a job with Boots the Chemist, where one of his duties was window display. His first published work appeared in March 1923 in Boots' staff magazine, *The Beacon*. By 1924 he had returned to the Nottingham School of Art on a full-time art scholarship.

It was around 1923 that he was spotted by a D. C. Thomson talent scout and offered a position as a staff artist with the firm. He moved to Dundee in 1925. The Scottish publisher had recently started a line of boys' story papers which were published weekly. The first was *Adventure* (which began in September 1921), and this had been followed by *Rover* (March 1922) and *Wizard* (September 1922). Eventually, there would be two more: *Skipper* (September 1930) and *Hotspur* (September 1933); collectively they became known as 'The Big Five'. D. C. Thomson was always looking for artists to supply front page drawings and paintings, title illustrations and various small pictures and jokes which helped to break up the text.

Even in those early days Watkins's three main talents were immediately obvious: he had a flair for the dramatic, his work seizing the reader's attention; he was able to convey humour; and he could draw extremely well indeed. The majority of his art managed to convey all three of these attributes and it was exactly what the successful and expanding company was looking for.

Watkins's first comic strip was 'P.C.99' (usually drawn by another

Willie's trademark was an upturned bucket; it served as a stage for his homespun philosophising. © D.C. Thomson & Co. Ltd.

artist, Chic Gordon) which appeared in *The Rover Midget Comic*, published free with *The Rover* on 11 February 1933. Three years later he was contributing small, six-picture strips to the pages of *Adventure*. One of these was 'Percy Vere and His Trying Tricks'; the other, in 1937, was 'Wandering Willie, the Wily Explorer'. Also during the 1930s he supplied many black and white illustrations to text stories appearing in *Topical Times* (1919–40), a Thomson paper which catered more to male adults than schoolboys.

On 8 March 1936, D. C. Thomson began to include a comic supplement entitled the *Fun Section* with its newspaper, the *Sunday Post*. From the start Watkins was given two picture strips to do: 'Oor Wullie' (Our Willie) and 'The Broons' (The Browns). Both were in the tradition of the type of comic strip that had been so popular in the United States, where the idea for a newspaper supplement was said to have originated. 'Oor Wullie', which occupied the important front page position, was about the day-to-day adventures of a mischievous young lad with spiked hair who dressed in dungarees. The Broons were a tightly knit Scottish family and provided a weekly soap opera which held its readership in thrall. The two features are still running. Until the 1970s the artwork remained that of Dudley Watkins, his drawings being reprinted for some years after his death.

The success of the *Fun Section* was an indication to D. C. Thomson that a national weekly comic was viable. R. D. Low, managing editor of

This Story Tells How Bully Bates

Took On A Lot When He Took Wull's Skates.

On 8 March 1936, D. C. Thomson began to include with its weekly newspaper, *The Sunday Post*, a comic supplement entitled the *Fun Section*. Dudley Watkins's front page contribution was 'Our Wullie'. Each year these pages were collected together and reprinted in the biennial 'Oor Wullie' book (1941 onwards). The page shown here was drawn in the late Thirties and was reprinted in the first book; it is interesting to compare it with the later, more accomplished, version a few pages on. © D.C. Thomson & Co. Ltd.

'The Broons', which also appeared in the *Fun Section*, was some of Dudley Watkins's finest work. Aimed at a mature readership, its warm, accurate portrayal of a closely knit Scottish family, complete with Gaelic speech, was masterful. It ranks as one of the finest comic features produced in Britain during the Forties and Fifties.
© D.C. Thomson & Co. Ltd.

A

children's publications, took charge of a production team mostly seconded from the story papers and which included the appointed editor, Albert Barnes, previously chief sub-editor on *The Wizard* and *The Hotspur*. The new weekly was named *The Dandy Comic* and was launched on 4 December 1937. Following the success of his work for the new *Fun Section* of the *Sunday Post*, Dudley Watkins was commissioned to draw some of the features: 'Desperate Dan', 'Our Gang' and 'Smarty Grandpaw'.

The most important of these was Desperate Dan, a cowboy with ten-gallon hat and permanent heavy stubble on his square chin. Dan was *tough*. He shaved with a blow-torch; swung bulls around his head by their tails; carried his horse when it got too tired to carry him and eschewed the use of a hammer by spitting nails into wood through his teeth. During the Second World War (which he could surely have won singlehandedly!), he drank the Channel to leave enemy submarines high and dry, and hurled boulders from Britain to Berlin with one swing of his arm.

Editor Albert Barnes and Dudley Watkins at one time lived but four

HI, TAM! GIE'S A LICHT!
LOOK! PAW'S GETTIN' A LICHT FOR HIS PIPE, FRAE OUTSIDE!
THANKS, TAM!
PUFF-DRAW-PUFF
AYE! THAT'S TAM THE LEERIE ~ A RARE AULD CHAP. LOOK, HE'S LETTIN' THE BAIRNS HAE A SHOTTIE AT LICHTIN' THE LAMPS!
MY TURN AT THE NEXT LAMP!
MAN, THE AULD LAD'S 77 ON FRIDAY, AN' HE'S RETIRIN'. HE'LL NO' BE ON THE LAMPS AGAIN.
AYE, HE LIVES BY HIMSEL', TAE.
WHIT ABOOT MAKIN' HIM A CAKE FOR HIS BIRTHDAY~AN' HAVIN' HIM UP HERE ON FRIDAY?
OH, HE'D LIKE THAT, MAW!
THURSDAY
OOH! THE CAKE LOOKS LOVELY. NICE AN' BROWN!
WELL, I'LL SOON HAE THE 'ICIN' READY!
ICING SUGAR
I'M COUNTIN' OOT SEVENTY-SEVEN CANDLES.
THIS IS TAE DAE WI' THE CAKE TAE, BUT IT'S MADE O' WOOD!
WHIT FOR?
FRIDAY EVENING
COME AWA' IN, TAM. WE'VE GOT A SURPRISE FOR YE!
BRING YER POLE WI' YE!
WHIT? FOR ME? OH, THAT'S FELL GOOD O' YE!
HA-HA! SEVENTY-SEVEN CANDLES ON A CAKE ON A HOME-MADE LAMP-POST!
HAPPY BIRTHDAY TO YOU— HAPPY BIRTHDAY TO YOU!
FOR HE'S A JOLLY GOOD LEERIE—
HOW ARE YE TAE BLAW THEM OOT, TAM?
DUDLEY D. WATKINS

DESPERATE DAN
WAKE UP, DAN! IT'S TIME YOU WENT HOME! I'VE GOT TO SHUT THE PARK GATES!
SMAKE
SNORE
GEE! I'LL HAVE TO WAKE HIM UP SOMEHOW, OR HE'D SOCK ME TOMORROW IF I LOCKED HIM IN THE PARK ALL NIGHT!
SNOOZE
Z-Z-Z
GOSH! HE'S STILL SLEEPING!
CONK!
Z-Z-Z
I'LL TRY A SOCK ON THE JAW! HE MIGHT FEEL THAT!
PLEASANT DREAMS
GOSH! I'VE WAKENED HIM!
BIFF!
YAWN
GEE, DAN! THE BRISTLES ON YOUR CHIN HAVE MADE MY HAND BLEED!
SO YOU TRIED TO WAKE ME UP EH?
AW GEE! DAN!—DON'T LOOK AT ME LIKE THAT,—ER, IT'S TIME FOR ME TO LOCK THE PARK GATES—I GUESS I'M SURE SORRY I HIT YOU, DAN! I SHOULDN'T HAVE DONE IT DAN—!!
KNOCK
COME HERE YOU!! I'M GOING TO GIVE YOU SOMETHING!!
AW-GOSH! HE'S GOING TO GIVE ME A GOOD BELTING—THAT'S WHAT IT IS!—I'LL GET UP THIS TREE!!
HUH! I'LL SOON GET YOU DOWN OUTTA THAT TREE!
AW GEE, DAN! HELP!!!
DUMBBELL!!!—I ONLY WANTED TO GIVE YOU THIS STICKING PLASTER FOR YOUR KNUCKLES—I HAVEN'T SHAVED THIS MORNING!
SWOOSH

Above and over page
Desperate Dan made his first appearance in No. 1 of *The Dandy Comic*, 4 December 1937, in the pictures shown above. He still appears today, 52 years on, promoted to the front page. Dudley Watkins drew him for 32 years. Throughout the Forties, Watkins developed Dan's physique: his chest became barrel-shaped; his jaw more pronounced. He became less Desperate and more Dan the British Superman.
© D. C. Thomson & Co. Ltd.

houses away from each other and it was said by Barnes's widow, Dorothy, that Desperate Dan was a particular favourite of both men. 'The two of them used to spend hours and hours working on the character,' she said. As a result, Dan gradually evolved from the simple creation he was in 1937 to the more fully rounded and multi-faceted character he became in later years. Dorothy Barnes also claimed that Dan's huge chin was modelled on that of her husband. Dudley Watkins drew Desperate Dan for more than 2,000 issues of the *Dandy* and the character still appears today, a half-century on, impeccably drawn by Charles Grigg in a style that owes everything to Watkins.

The successor to the *Dandy* was *The Beano Comic* which began publication on 30 July 1938. Considering Watkins's other commitments, editor George Mooney was fortunate in being able to commission any work from him, even though it was only a simple one-page picture strip. But this strip was destined to be one of the classics

A similar feature to 'Our Gang' was drawn by Watkins for *The Beano Comic* in 1938. 'Lord Snooty' had the better premise of the young lord who rejected the aristocracy for the company of street urchins: it also had the advantage of originality. 'Our Gang' invited comparison with the cinema and suffered as a result. This early 'Lord Snooty' page is dated 3 November 1945 (No. 270). The feature is still running today after more than half a century. © D.C. Thomson & Co. Ltd.

Funny Fellows, Every One—Join Our Gang and Have Some Fun.

OUR GANG

Spot The Pup | Alfalfa Switzer | Scotty Beckett | Darla Hood | Billy Thomas | Porky Lee | Patsy May | Spanky McFarland | Buckwheat Thomas

All these boys and girls play in the famous Hal Roach films of "Our Gang," and appear here by courtesy of M-G-M.

1—There was a big meeting in the Gang Clubhouse the other day, with Buckwheat Thomas, Scotty Beckett, Alfalfa Switzer, Billy Thomas, Darla Hood, Spanky McFarland, and Porky Lee all present. Even Spot the Pup was there, and everybody except Alfalfa was trying to think of something the Gang could do. Alfalfa folded his arms and thought of nothing. You see, he sprained his brain when he was learning the A B C, and he hasn't done any thinking since!

2—Then in came Baby Patsy May with a proper brainwave. "Let's make a fire engine," she said. Billy Thomas got so excited at the notion that she hit Alfalfa on the head with the mallet. But nobody noticed this, because it made the same sound as if the mallet had hit the wooden box. Porky was dreaming of food as usual, and his dreams came true, for his hair was ironed out by Scotty's meaty feet.

Above: see previous page for the reason Snooty's so popular! © D.C. Thomson & Co. Ltd.

Below:
Watkins's main feature for *The Dandy Comic* in 1937 was 'Our Gang', based upon the street kids who had earned their popularity in the films made by Hal Roach Studios. Watkins strove for – and achieved – accurate likenesses. © D.C. Thomson & Co. Ltd.

Opposite
D. C. Thomson's third new comic in fewer years was *The Magic Comic* (22 July 1939). One of the main features was 'Peter Piper' by Watkins. © D.C. Thomson & Co. Ltd.

Statues wake up at the toot — Of Peter Piper's magic flute!

PETER PIPER

PICKING PEOPLE OUT OF PICKLES

Beside the statues in the park
Walks Peter Piper, a bright spark.
But Peter's due some nasty shocks,
For two toughs wait to give him socks.

Pete passes by The bullies pounce!
His chin upon the ground they bounce,
And tug his hair and pull his ears—
But help's at hand, so dry your tears!

For, hearing all the sounds of strife,
A stony statue wakes to life!
It's Pan the Piper, and he wipes
His eyes—then tootles on his pipes!

His music rings out wild and clear
And—look out, kids! What have we here?
To life the Samson statue wakes!
With rage and wrath he simply quakes.

He throws the stone with all his might
And gives the bullies such a fright
That Peter now can dodge away—
Then Samson leaps into the fray!

The tough guys think they're in a war,
For Samson gives them both what for!
And meanwhile Pan jumps to his feet
And gives his set of pipes to Pete.

"One toot—and statues wake!" says he.
And while the yelling bullies flee,
Young Peter tootles—"Roo-too-too!"
To see if what Pan says is true.

It works! For Cupid, full of go,
Fits two stone arrows to his bow.
Then—twang! The archer's aim is good.
He's punctured both the bullies rude!

Back in their place the statues stand.
You'd think they'd never moved a hand.
But pipeless Pan is winking now.
Will Pete have fun? He will—and how!

of British comics: 'Lord Snooty', the young aristocrat in the top hat and Eton suit, who would rather fraternise with street urchins than the Toffs of Bunkerton Hall.

Watkins's early drawings of Snooty and his gang were crude, but gradually his style matured so that by the 1940s 'Lord Snooty' was looking what it was: a superior piece of work by an accomplished and professional comic artist. The same was true of his work in the *Dandy* ('Desperate Dan' and 'Our Gang') and to the *Fun Section* capers of 'Oor Wullie' and 'The Broons'. One commentator has said of Watkins, 'As an illustrator, he was among the first comic artists to capture the cheeky makeshift world of children in a way that was neither patronising nor sentimental.' This assessment was never more accurate than when applied to 'Lord Snooty'.

After the *Dandy* and the *Beano*, D. C. Thomson launched yet another new weekly in a similar vein. Entitled *The Magic Comic*, it was aimed at a slightly younger age group. Due, apparently, to the paper shortages of the Second World War, the *Magic* lasted for only 80 issues. For this Watkins drew 'Peter Piper' (for the entire run) and 'Gulliver' (20 issues).

Some of Dudley Watkins's finest work was for the picture stories 'The Shipwrecked Circus' and 'Jimmy and his Magic Patch'. The former began in *Beano* No. 200 dated 27 February 1943, the story of a small band of circus troupers who made their home on a desert island when their ship sank in a storm. 'Jimmy and his Magic Patch' was about a schoolboy with a patch sewn into the seat of his trousers by a gypsy he had helped; the patch had been cut from a magic carpet and could whisk the youth back into the past at a mere wish. The first story of Jimmy Watson and the Magic Patch appeared in the *Beano* on New Year's Day 1944. Told in weekly adventures of 16 pictures, it was primarily these two features that established Watkins's reputation not only as an excellent 'funnies' artist, but also as a first-rate 'adventure' artist.

By the mid-1940s, Dudley Watkins's work was confident, mature and skilful. In 1946 he began to sign his work, a concession perhaps from his employers that he was acknowledged as their most important artist. The signature 'Dudley D. Watkins' was clear and distinct and noted by millions; it led to him being the best-known of all British comic artists.

Throughout the 1940s Watkins continued to be principal artist on important features. These ranged

'Gulliver', in prose, was supplemented by a small self-contained comic strip. From *The Magic Comic* 28 December, 1940. (No. 76).

The Sunday toast of the 'Sunday Post'—Oor Wullie!

Oh, jings! Whit has Oor Wullie done?
The poor wee chap is on the run!

But though the germs catch him at last,
They're ower late—the party's past!

Above
When this page was published, Watkins had been drawing 'Oor Wullie' for 11 years and had become extremely accomplished. © D. C. Thomson & Co. Ltd.

Opposite
No. 1 of *The Topper*, D. C. Thomson's first post-war tabloid, which was hugely successful. 'Mickey the Monkey' on the front page is by Watkins. © D.C. Thomson & Co. Ltd.

The first issue of *The Beezer*, in which Watkins embellished the front page with 'Ginger', a lad similar in appearance to 'Oor Wullie'. © D.C. Thomson & Co. Ltd.

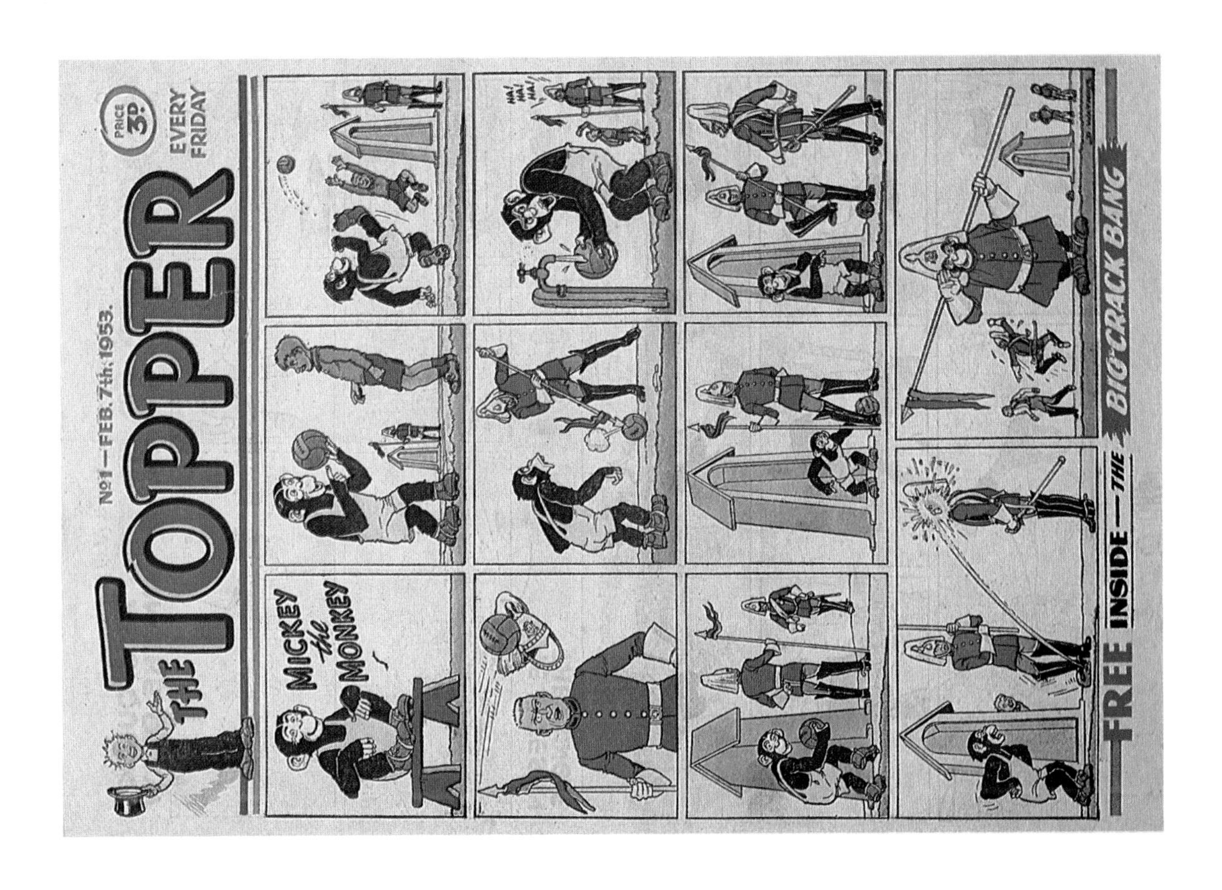
THE TOPPER
No1—FEB.7th.1953.
PRICE 3D
EVERY FRIDAY
MICKEY the MONKEY
HA! HA! HA!
FREE INSIDE—THE BIG CRACK BANG

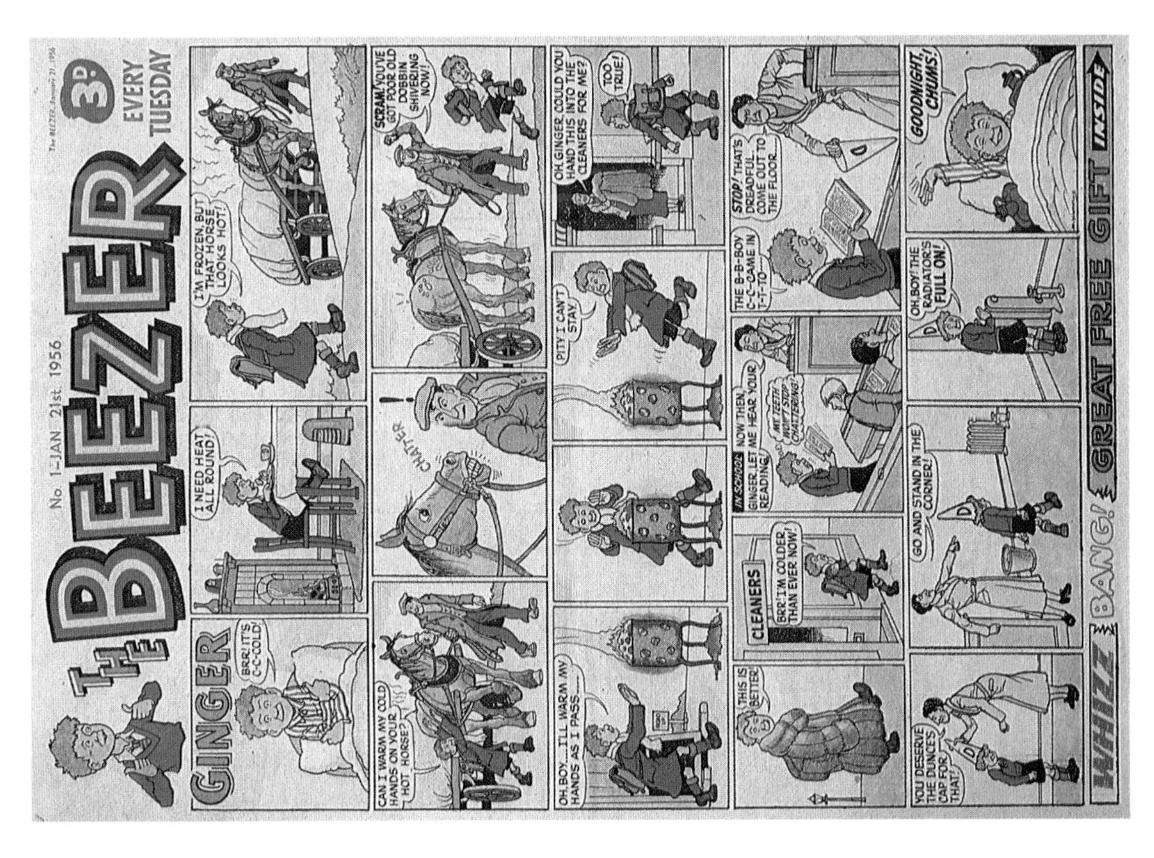
THE BEEZER
No 1—JAN 21st 1956
3D
EVERY TUESDAY
GINGER
BRR! IT'S C-C-COLD!
I NEED HEAT ALL ROUND!
I'M FROZEN, BUT THAT HORSE LOOKS HOT!
CAN I WARM MY COLD HANDS ON YOUR HOT HORSE?
CHAT-TER
SCRAM! YOU'VE GOT POOR OLD DOBBIN SHIVERING NOW!
OH, BOY... I'LL WARM MY HANDS AS I PASS....
PITY I CAN'T STAY!
OH, GINGER, COULD YOU HAND THIS INTO THE CLEANERS FOR ME?
TOO TRUE!
THIS IS BETTER!
CLEANERS
BRR! I'M COLDER THAN EVER NOW!
IN SCHOOL
NOW THEN, GINGER, LET ME HEAR YOUR READING!
MY TEETH WON'T STOP CHATTERING!
THE B-B-BOY C-C-CAME IN T-T-TO-
STOP! THAT'S DREADFUL! COME OUT TO THE FLOOR.
YOU DESERVE THE DUNCE'S CAP FOR THAT!
GO AND STAND IN THE CORNER!
OH, BOY! THE RADIATOR'S FULL ON!
GOODNIGHT, CHUMS!
WHIZZ BANG! GREAT FREE GIFT INSIDE

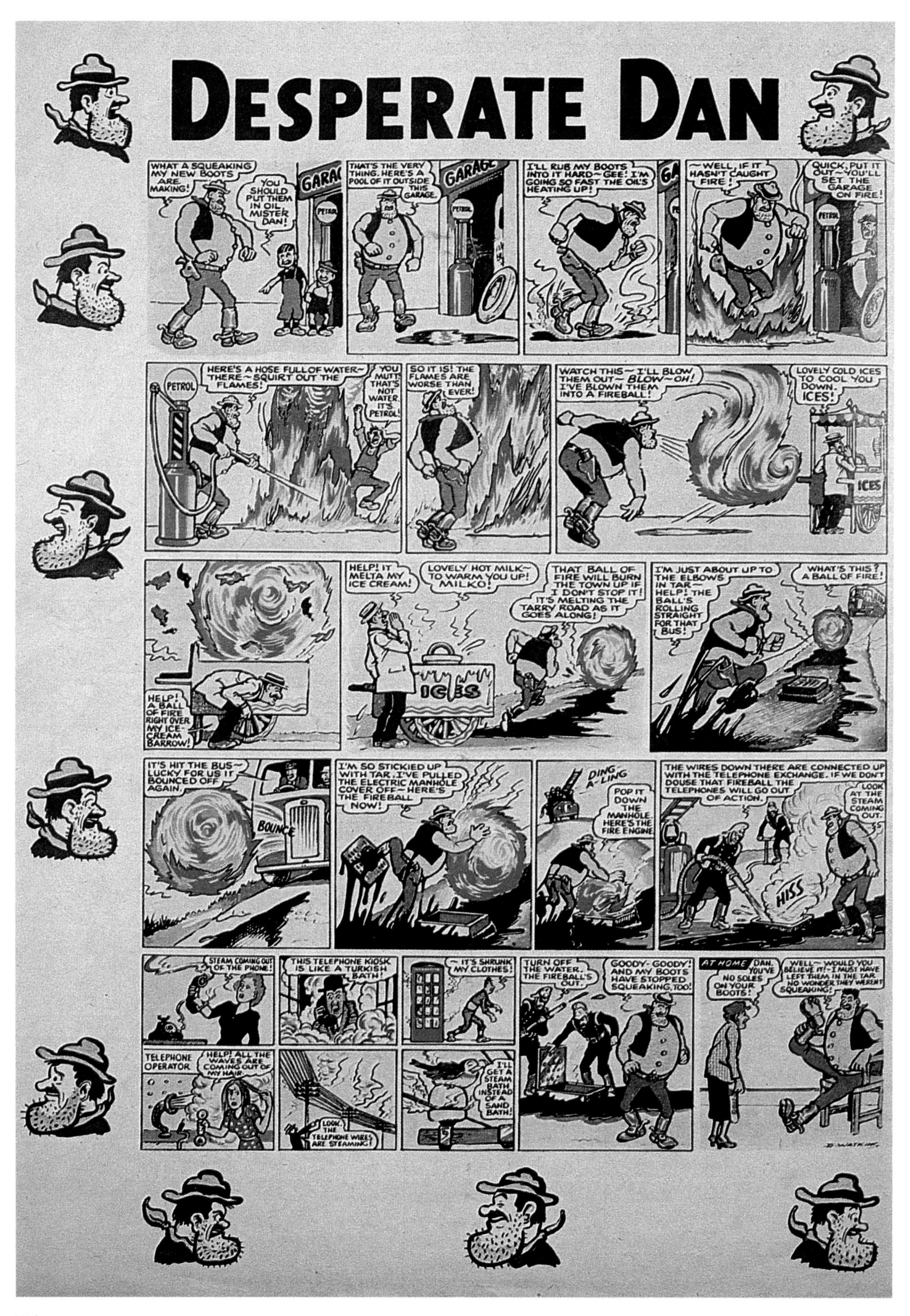
DESPERATE DAN
WHAT A SQUEAKING MY NEW BOOTS ARE MAKING!
YOU SHOULD PUT THEM IN OIL MISTER DAN!
GARAG
THAT'S THE VERY THING. HERE'S A POOL OF IT OUTSIDE THIS GARAGE.
GARAGE
PETROL
I'LL RUB MY BOOTS INTO IT HARD~GEE! I'M GOING SO FAST THE OIL'S HEATING UP!
~WELL, IF IT HASN'T CAUGHT FIRE!
QUICK, PUT IT OUT~YOU'LL SET THE GARAGE ON FIRE!
PETROL
HERE'S A HOSE FULL OF WATER~THERE~SQUIRT OUT THE FLAMES!
YOU MUTT! THAT'S NOT WATER, IT'S PETROL!
SO IT IS! THE FLAMES ARE WORSE THAN EVER!
WATCH THIS~I'LL BLOW THEM OUT~BLOW~OH! I'VE BLOWN THEM INTO A FIREBALL!
LOVELY COLD ICES TO COOL YOU DOWN. ICES!
ICES
HELP! A BALL OF FIRE RIGHT OVER MY ICE-CREAM BARROW!
HELP! IT MELTA MY ICE CREAM!
LOVELY HOT MILK~TO WARM YOU UP! MILKO!
THAT BALL OF FIRE WILL BURN THE TOWN UP IF I DON'T STOP IT! IT'S MELTING THE TARRY ROAD AS IT GOES ALONG!
ICES
I'M JUST ABOUT UP TO THE ELBOWS IN TAR~HELP! THE BALL'S ROLLING STRAIGHT FOR THAT BUS!
WHAT'S THIS? A BALL OF FIRE!
IT'S HIT THE BUS~LUCKY FOR US IT BOUNCED OFF AGAIN.
BOUNCE
I'M SO STICKIED UP WITH TAR, I'VE PULLED THE ELECTRIC MANHOLE COVER OFF~HERE'S THE FIREBALL NOW!
DING-A-LING
POP IT DOWN THE MANHOLE. HERE'S THE FIRE ENGINE
THE WIRES DOWN THERE ARE CONNECTED UP WITH THE TELEPHONE EXCHANGE. IF WE DON'T DOUSE THAT FIREBALL THE TELEPHONES WILL GO OUT OF ACTION.
LOOK AT THE STEAM COMING OUT.
HISS
STEAM COMING OUT OF THE PHONE!
THIS TELEPHONE KIOSK IS LIKE A TURKISH BATH!
~IT'S SHRUNK MY CLOTHES!
TELEPHONE OPERATOR
HELP! ALL THE WAVES ARE COMING OUT OF MY HAIR.
LOOK, THE TELEPHONE WIRES ARE STEAMING!
I'LL GET A STEAM BATH INSTEAD OF A SAND BATH!
TURN OFF THE WATER. THE FIREBALL'S OUT.
GOODY-GOODY! AND MY BOOTS HAVE STOPPED SQUEAKING, TOO!
AT HOME
DAN, YOU'VE NO SOLES ON YOUR BOOTS!
WELL~WOULD YOU BELIEVE IT!~I MUST HAVE LEFT THEM IN THE TAR. NO WONDER THEY WEREN'T SQUEAKING!

Dudley D. Watkins

Watkins had become very accomplished in eleven years of drawing 'The Broons'. The detail within this page is extraordinary for a weekly comic. © D. C. Thomson & Co. Ltd.

from adventure – as depicted in 'Strang the Terrible' (*Beano*: 1944) and 'Six Brands for Bonnie Prince Charlie' (*Beano*: 1945) – to humorous adventure in 'Lazy Larry' (*Dandy*: 1945) and 'Danny Longlegs' (*Dandy*: 1945) – to pure comedy in 'Our Teacher's a Walrus!' (*Dandy*: 1947). Both 'Strang the Terrible' and 'Our Teacher's a Walrus!' had been popular features in story papers some years prior to Watkins's successful resurrection of them in picture form.

It was in the late 1940s and early 1950s that Watkins was commissioned to draw adventure serials, for D. C. Thomson's large-circulation newspaper, *The People's Journal*. Between 1947 and 1953 he drew 'Wild Young Dirky', 'Kidnapped', 'Catriona', 'Oliver Twist', 'Treasure Island', 'Robinson Crusoe', 'Gordon the Gypsy' and 'The Three Musketeers'. Some of these were successful enough to be reprinted in book form and in Thomson's first post-war

Opposite
Desperate Dan in full colour from *The Dandy-Beano Summer Special* (1963). Dan's encounter with a fireball is typical of the kind of set produced on a regular basis by Watkins – slightly odd, but full of interest and fun. © D.C. Thomson & Co. Ltd.

JIMMY AND HIS MAGIC PATCH

1—" Boy, oh boy!" chuckled Jimmy Watson as he stepped out of the stationer's shop with a handful of fireworks. " What wouldn't I do to Guy Fawkes with this little lot!" It was the fifth of November and Jimmy had decided that he wasn't going to let that date pass without some fun. " There must have been real fun on the day of the gunpowder plot," thought Jimmy. " I wish I had been there."

2—Swoosh! Jimmy's Magic Patch carried him through space once more and Jimmy soon found his wish granted. He found himself beside a number of gunpowder barrels. But that wasn't the big surprise. On the other side of the barrels sat the men plotting to blow up the Houses of Parliament! They were just as surprised as Jimmy and leapt to their feet. " Catch him," roared the leader. " He's probably heard all our plans."

3—The sinister-looking cloaked figures made a dash for Jimmy. The quick-witted lad acted. He knew what the penalty for overhearing the plot would be if he was caught. A hefty shove sent a large barrel rolling in front of the conspirators. This caused them a spot of bother, because they were unable to get out of the way in time and were bowled over like ninepins by the heavy gunpowder barrel.

4—Jimmy made the most of the opportunity and headed for a flight of steps, but just as he neared the door at the top he stopped in horror. Another cloaked figure opened the door and held his rapier at Jimmy's throat. He had heard the uproar and appeared at a bad time for Jimmy. The lad was trapped! At once the other plotters were on him and he was helpless.

5—At an order from the leader one of them fetched over a large empty gunpowder barrel. Jimmy was forced into this and one of the conspirators fixed the lid in place. Jimmy Watson was scared, and he had every right to be. What were the sinister conspirators going to do with him? Suddenly he felt the barrel being moved. Through the bunghole of the barrel he saw that it was being lifted with others into a cart in the street.

6—Jimmy wondered how he could tell people of his presence in the barrel. Suddenly he felt one of the cannon crackers in his pocket. " The very thing," he thought to himself. " Where's my matches?" Soon he fished them out and, striking one, lit the fuse of the cannon cracker. The cart was just passing one of the city watchmen. Jimmy put his arm out through the bunghole of the barrel and dropped the firework.

7—The cracker exploded with a terrific bang that seemed to rock even the barrel where Jimmy crouched with his fingers crossed. It certainly shook the watchman. He was given a terrific fright and jumped backwards rather hurriedly—into a nearby horse-trough! Jimmy wondered if the dazed man would realise that the cartload of barrels was not all it should be. The cart rumbled on and soon they were near the House of Commons.

8—Once more he felt the barrel being lifted and when it was put down and the lid taken off Jimmy was pulled out. He found himself in the cellar below the House of Commons. While the conspirators fixed the gunpowder barrels and the fuse, Jimmy was bound to one of the barrels. His hands were left free, but the knots were placed well out of reach. The conspirators lit the fuse and waved a mocking farewell.

9—But Jimmy did not mean to be blown up! Oh, no! A scheme was already forming in Jimmy's agile brain. Swiftly, for the fuse was burning low, he took the lighted candle the traitors had left, out of the bottle and put in its place a large rocket. Jimmy lit the fuse with the candle and directed the rocket towards the small barred window just above ground level. The fuse seemed to take ages to burn.

10—Suddenly sparks flew from the rocket and it swooshed through the barred window. By this time the watchman Jimmy had scared with the cannon cracker had gathered other members of the watch and followed the cart. They were more than just a little surprised when the rocket swooshed over their heads. It took them but a few seconds to realise that something was amiss in the cellar. Quickly they forced their way into it.

11—Jimmy gasped with relief as one of the men stamped out the gunpowder fuse and he was untied. The House of Commons had been saved. It was Jimmy's timely warning that had saved the King's life. Jimmy didn't get time to get much thanks for his deed, however. No sooner was he untied than the Magic Patch brought him back to modern times once more. With a slight bump he landed in the street near his home.

12—Later that night Jimmy joined his pals and erected a guy. The flashing and banging of squibs and the swooshing of rockets as they soared into the sky reminded Jimmy of his exciting adventure. His pals threw fireworks at the guy and Jimmy did the same. His only wish was that it had been the real conspirators he was throwing squibs at. He contented himself with the thought that he had spoiled their cowardly plot.

'There must have been some real fun on the day of the Gunpowder Plot,' thought Jimmy Watson. 'I wish I'd been there.' Which was all that was needed for the Magic Patch to whisk the schoolboy back to that dramatic day in the Houses of Parliament. Watkins used a mere 12 pictures to draw a story that had instant appeal for its young audience. From *The Beano Comic* 3 November 1945 (No. 270). © D.C. Thomson & Co. Ltd.

THE SHIPWRECKED CIRCUS

1—Clang! clang! went the bell on the deck of the s.s. " Margo." The " Margo," or what was left of it, was the home of the chums of Samson's Circus, shipwrecked many months ago when the " Margo " had broken in two after running aground on a reef off Crusoe Island during a storm in the South Seas. To-day was Christmas morning and Samson, the owner and strong man of the Circus, was tolling the ship's bell to waken his pals—Danny, the young acrobat, Gloopy, the dwarf, and Horace, the educated ape. Young Trixie, the circus tight-rope walker, was up already preparing breakfast. " Merry Christmas, kids!" boomed Samson, then seeing some natives clambering aboard, added with a grin, " Show a leg, kids! Here come Chief Umpala and his men."

2—" Whoopee!" yelled Gloopy, nearly falling out of his hammock in his haste to greet the dusky warriors of Crusoe Island who had become such close friends of the chums of the Shipwrecked Circus. " Good old Umpala!" grinned Danny, warmly shaking the old chief's hand. " Merry Christmas!" Breakfast was soon forgotten when the natives opened the sacks they carried and handed out gifts to the chums. For Samson and his pals had taught the natives all about Christmas and the white man's custom of giving gifts on the 25th of December. In their turn, the chums opened their store of trading goods in the hold and gave Christmas gifts to the natives—shiny top hats, umbrellas and many other things that the natives had never seen before.

3—So pleased were the chums with their new gifts that they promised to make a plum pudding for the natives' Christmas dinner. As the warriors began to return to their village on the shore, Samson, using the biggest pot he could find, started to make a huge plum pudding with supplies from the ship's stores.

4—So delicious did the Christmas pudding taste when it was cooked, that Gloopy, the dwarf, offered to eat it all himself—and it weighed nearly half a ton! It was dinner-time—time to take the giant pudding to Umpala's village on the shore. So Samson dressed up in a Father Christmas costume which Trixie had made.

5—The chums then climbed into a brand-new native war canoe, another of Umpala's Christmas gifts to them, and started paddling across the bay, towing a raft on which was the giant pudding. " Boy, oh, boy!" grinned Danny. " Just wait till Umpala and his pals taste this pudding! Why, it's the best—" Danny's grin faded. " Look out!" he cried. " Here comes a sawfish!"

6—The monster was charging straight at the war canoe. " Hang on tightly!" yelled Samson, and with a mighty stroke of his paddle sent the canoe shooting forward. The huge fish missed the canoe, but its " saw," sharp as a razor, sliced clean through the two-rope. Again the monster charged. Thud!—its " saw " struck the underside of the raft and lifted one end into the air.

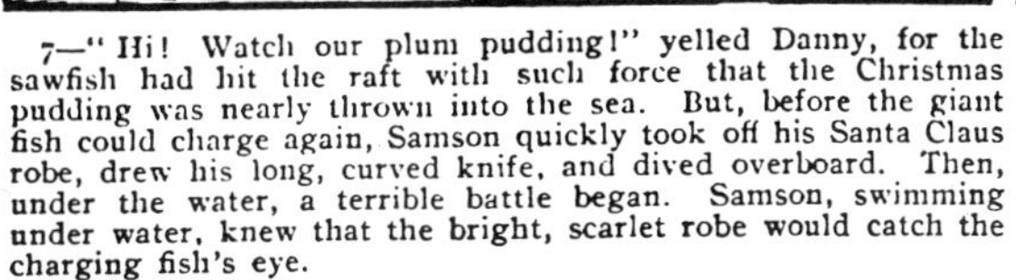
7—"Hi! Watch our plum pudding!" yelled Danny, for the sawfish had hit the raft with such force that the Christmas pudding was nearly thrown into the sea. But, before the giant fish could charge again, Samson quickly took off his Santa Claus robe, drew his long, curved knife, and dived overboard. Then, under the water, a terrible battle began. Samson, swimming under water, knew that the bright, scarlet robe would catch the charging fish's eye.

8—Trixie and Danny saw the monster dart towards the scarlet robe. A second later they saw the wicked looking "saw" tear into the cloth. At the same time Samson dodged aside and plunged his knife into the sawfish as it shot past. The keen blade found its mark. The great fish twitched for a few moments, then was still. The monster was dead. The Christmas pudding had been saved. It took only a few minutes to tie the tow-rope to the canoe once more.

9—When the strong man came shooting to the surface, he pointed to the corpse of the sawfish floating on the water. "We'll take this sardine to Umpala," he grinned. "It gives me an idea." Before Trixie and Danny could ask what the idea was, Samson had started to swim to the shore, pushing the dead sawfish in front of him. The natives had seen that underwater fight, and they cheered when Samson walked ashore.

10—Umpala's dusky warriors were so pleased to see their white friends safe and sound that they carried them shoulder-high to the little village on the edge of the jungle. Half a dozen burly warriors carried the giant Christmas pudding along behind. And then the strong man dressed the dead monster in the Santa Claus robes, and, after breaking off the razor-sharp "saw," used it to slice up the huge pudding! And what a feed those natives had!

11—Trixie, Danny and Gloopy carried platefuls of the delicious pudding to the villagers as they sat round in a huge circle. Many of the natives, especially the youngsters, had three or four helpings, until at last the huge pudding was finished. Then came the treat which Samson had planned to give the villagers. The circus strong man fixed up a home-made roundabout with old arm-chairs, toy cars and message baskets from the ship.

12—Papa Umo, the oldest native on the island, whizzed round in the biggest boiling pot in the village! Meanwhile Horace had made a coconut-shy and Gloopy a hoop-la stall, and there the black warriors enjoyed all the fun of the fair. Trixie and Danny put on a show of their own, and when the fun was over, the chums of the circus all agreed that it was the happiest Christmas they had spent for many years.

The characters in Watkins's other classic picture strip, 'The Shipwrecked Circus', had first been introduced in 1928, in D. C. Thomson's story paper *The Adventure*. Watkins drew the picture version's 13 opening episodes. This Christmas adventure appeared in *The Beano Comic* 28 December 1946 (No. 300). © D.C. Thomson & Co. Ltd.

Watkins was equally brilliant at straight adventure. He was responsible for the dust-jacket and interior illustrations for a hard-cover book, 'Morgyn the Mighty' (1951), reprints of some of the loinclothed hero's best adventures from the story paper *The Rover*. © D.C. Thomson & Co. Ltd.

comic, *The Topper*, launched on 7 February 1953.

The Topper was produced as a tabloid when tabloids seemed to be going out of fashion. It was in that same year that the Amalgamated Press axed several of its tabloid titles and reduced some of the new comics, such as *Lion* and *TV Fun*, to half the size. But *The Topper* was a success, proving – if any proof were needed – that it was not the format but the content that was important. Dudley Watkins's main contribution to the new comic was 'Mickey the Monkey' which appeared on the front page. His real tour-de-force, though, was on the back page where the *People's Journal* serials were being reprinted. These had been excellent in black

Morgyn dug his fingers desperately into the sand as the octopus began pulling him into the sea.

To prevent themselves from sinking into the swamp, the savages wore broad plates of hide on their feet.

and white; in colour they were magnificent. The reprints began with 'Treasure Island' and continued with 'Kidnapped', 'Robinson Crusoe', 'Wild Young Dirky' and 'Prester John'.

D. C. Thomson also published hardcover books, reprinting Watkins's work from *The People's Journal*. These began to be issued in 1948 with 'Kidnapped' and, subsequently, 'Oliver Twist' (1949), 'Treasure Island' (1950, reprinted 1959) and 'Robinson Crusoe' (1952). The firm also published in hardcover 'Morgyn the Mighty', which contained text stories accompanied by several full-page illustrations by Watkins.

The Topper having firmly established itself, the Dundee firm

Robert Louis Stevenson's 'Treasure Island' was published by D. C. Thomson in 1950. Watkins supplied the illustrations two to a page, 122 pictures in all. It first appeared in the weekly *The People's Journal* (1949); in 1953 it was reprinted in full colour on the back page of *The Topper*. © D.C. Thomson & Co. Ltd.

launched *The Beezer* on 21 January 1956. Again, Watkins's work was featured on page one with 'Ginger', a similar but slightly older version of 'Oor Wullie' which he was still drawing for the *Sunday Post*. He did little other work for *The Beezer*, except for the occasional commissions in later years for *The Beezer Annual*.

Dudley Watkins had always been religious and throughout his life had taken an active role in the church. He gave talks on various aspects of his belief and was a member of the Church of Christ in Dundee, where he used his artistic talents to help the movement by drawing mission calendars and other material. He once proclaimed it his ambition to produce an illustrated version of the Bible. From 1956 he produced 'William the Warrior' for the Worldwide Evangeli-

The Fate of Israel Hands

93

Something sang like an arrow through the air. Jim felt a blow and then a sharp pang, and there he was, pinned by the shoulder to the mast. In the horrid pain and surprise of the moment—Jim could scarcely say it was by his own will, and it was without a conscious aim—both his pistols went off, and both escaped out of his hands. They did not fall alone ; with a choked cry, the mutineer loosed his grasp upon the shrouds, and owing to the cant of the vessel, plunged head first into the water.

Hands rose once to the surface in a lather of foam and blood, and then sank again for good. Jim's first thought was to pluck forth the knife that pinned his shoulder to the mast ; but his nerve failed him and he desisted with a violent shudder. Oddly enough, that very shudder did the business. The knife held him by a mere pinch of skin, and this the shudder tore away. Jim regained the deck. He could see Hands lying stone-dead on the clean sand, with the quick fishes steering over him.

A simply superb 'Desperate Dan' page published on 6 June 1953 (No. 602). This special number of *The Dandy* sent Dan to the Queen's Coronation. It is a classic page with Dan perfectly in character, and in which he takes considerable liberties with Big Ben's clock tower.
© D.C. Thomson & Co. Ltd.

sation Crusade; these were comic strips published in small paper booklets and priced at one shilling. The lead character, William, was a remarkable look-alike of Jimmy, this time without his Magic Patch. A certain religious element was also evident in his work during the 1950s. 'The Giant Killer of Judah' (*Beezer Book:* 1960), 'Away in a Manger' (*Beezer Book*: 1961) and 'David' (*Sparky*: 1965).

Watkins lived in a large house named 'Winsterley' in Broughty Ferry, Scotland, and died of a heart attack while at work there on 20 August 1969. The legacy he left is still with us. If one man and his art could be said epitomise the comics of D. C. Thomson, it would be Dudley Watkins; his influence still can be seen 20 years after his death, and will no doubt continue for many years to come.

KEN REID

In the United Kingdom comic artists work for either the London-based Fleetway Publications (the comics of which were formerly published by IPC and the Amalgamated Press) or D. C. Thomson, with offices in Dundee. Few artists have worked for both, compelled by loyalty and 'gentlemen's agreements' to remain with one or the other company all of their working lives. Ken Reid (1919–87) was an exception: his career began with a provincial newspaper, moved on to the Amalgamated Press and then to D. C. Thomson where he drew some of the best-known characters of the 1950s. Following this he worked for Odhams Press, and his career came full circle when this company was taken over by IPC, which by then also owned the comics of the Amalgamated Press. A comic artist has to be very good indeed to be able to change his employer in this way; but then, Reid was not simply good – he was brilliant.

Ken Reid was born on 18 December 1919 in Manchester, the son of a father who was a manufacturing chemist and a mother who ran a ladies' and children's outfitters. A born artist, he drew constantly. When he was nine, doctors diagnosed that he had a tubercular hip and he was confined to bed for many months; at one time it was thought that he might never walk again. Each day throughout his illness he filled in the long, bed-ridden hours with drawing. Fortunately, he recovered and was able to return to school where he pursued his interest in art. When he left in 1932, at the age of 14, his abilities helped him to achieve a scholarship to Salford Art School where he spent the next four years.

After leaving the school in 1936 he established himself as a commercial artist but managed to scrape only a meagre living with various odd jobs around Manchester. Later, his father, acting as his agent, managed to secure him an interview with the art editor of the *Manchester Evening News* who said that he was thinking of starting a children's feature and was inviting various artists to suggest ideas. The result was 'The Adventures of Fudge the Elf' which Reid submitted in early 1938. Six weeks later his contribution was formally accepted and he was commissioned to write and draw 'Fudge' which appeared at the rate of three panels a day. The first 'Fudge' appeared in the *Manchester Evening News* on 7 April 1938. Reid wrote and drew eleven stories between 1938 and 1940 and the feature became enormously popular. A Fudge doll was a best-seller; Hodder and Stoughton and the London University Press issued books and the newspaper strip seemed set for a long run. But then came the war and Reid was called up to serve as a private in the Royal Army Service Corps;

Fudge the Elf and his friend Speck are shown here in an underwater sequence which appeared in 'Fudge and the Dragon' (*Manchester Evening News* 1946–7). When Fudge was created in 1938, Reid modelled his appearance on Mickey Mouse: witness the tight-fitting head garment with its distinctively-shaped facial surround.

Fudge was discontinued for the duration.

After the war Ken Reid returned to Fudge and this continued to be his main source of income until the early 1950s, when he decided to take on other work and contacted the Amalgamated Press. The AP immediately put him to work on 'Super Sam', an existing strip, and asked him to create a new feature, which he did, entitling it 'Foxy'. Both appeared in AP's long-running *Comic Cuts*. Unfortunately, the successful formula which had kept *Comic Cuts* in continuous publication since 1890 was not applicable to the new Elizabethan Age. After a few months of his first work being published, Reid received notice that the comic was to be discontinued. The last issue was dated 12 September 1953.

He decided to try another publisher, submitting a feature called 'Zooville' to Hulton, publishers of *Eagle*. Around the same time Reid's brother-in-law, who was an artist working for D. C. Thomson, publishers of *The Dandy* and *Beano*, informed his employers that Reid was looking for work. *The Beano* contacted him, asking if he'd like to do a new feature entitled 'Roger the Dodger'; when he agreed R. D. Low, managing editor, came to see him and look at some of the preliminary sketches Reid had done. The visual conception of Roger was agreed and Reid began to draw the set on a weekly basis. The first published appearance was on 18 April 1953.

Other commissions from D. C. Thomson soon followed: 'Angel Face', 'Grandpa' and 'Bing Bang Benny'.

Roger the Dodger made his first appearance in the *Beano* on 18 April 1953. This sequence is from the *Dandy-Beano Summer Special* (1963). © D.C. Thomson & Co. Ltd.

BING BANG BENNY
MIDNIGHT–
HEH-HEH!
TICK TICK
KEEP OUT– INJUN TERRITORY
I'M JUST POSTIN' A TIME-BOMB IN OLD BIG MOUTH HERE. THEM INJUNS HOLD A POW-WOW ROUND HIM TOMORROW, AN' THAT'S WHEN IT'LL GO OFF!
TICK TICK
BUT, AFTER BENNY HAS SNEAKED AWAY–
TICK TICK TICK
OH! UM-GOLLY!
YUM-YUM GOT WOODWORM IN TUM-TUM!
TICK TICK TICK
M-M-M! ME GOT UM GOOD IDEA!– PUSH YUM-YUM IN RIVER TO DROWN WOODWORM!
TICK TICK TICK
THERE! THEN ME HAUL YUM-YUM ASHORE TOMORROW IN TIME FOR POW-WOW!
BUT DURING THE NIGHT YUM-YUM GOES FOR A CRUISE–
SNAP
AND NEXT MORNING–
I'LL JUST SWIM OUT TO THAT ROCK AN' BACK TO GIVE ME AN APPETITE.
G-GOLLY! WH-WHAT'S THAT TICKIN' NOISE?
TICK-TICK TICK-TICK TICK
NO! IT CAN'T BE! YES! IT'S YUM-YUM'S
CLICK
TUM!
WOW!
BOOM
GLUB-GLUB! (GURGLE) GLUBBUB-GLUB (GULP) GLUBBUBUB - GLUB!
YOU'D NEED A DIVING SUIT TO HEAR WHAT BENNY'S SAYING, FOLKS– BUT IT WOULDN'T BE WORTH IT!

Opposite
This character was dangerously fascinated by high explosive. Here, Reid benefits from a strong and very funny script. It works because it combines a reasonable plan with the bad luck that life can bring, and results in perfect justice! Reid's cheeky-faced youngster is a superb foil.
© D.C. Thomson & Co. Ltd.

This is the first 'Frankie Stein' page from *Wham!* 11 July 1964. The new comic character, based on Mary Shelley's monster, is here the creation of Professor Cube of Mildew Manor and intended as a playmate for his son, Mickey. Reid's art was mature, crisp and clean; and note how detailed his drawings are.
© Fleetway Publications, London, 1989.

This 'Frankie Stein' page was published a few months after the one on page 125. Although Mickey has come to like his new friend, Professor Cube now regrets creating his monster and is determined to get rid of it. Reid has modified Frankie slightly, giving him a flat head and some wonderful comic expressions.
© Fleetway Publications, London, 1989.

Together with his commitment to 'Fudge', for the *Manchester Evening News*, and a competition drawing he regularly drew for the Irish edition of the *Sunday Express*, this kept him busier than ever. Reid continued to write and draw Fudge until 1961 when illness and pressure of other work combined to make him stop and the feature came to an end. After the war, three more 'Fudge' books were published by the London University Press; these contained reprints but also had some original work by Reid. All are avidly sought by collectors.

Ken Reid's most popular character was Jonah, a gormless, goofy goon created by George Mooney, the editor of *The Beano* at the time, and based on his wartime experience in the Navy. A sailor who only had to set foot on the deck of any ship to send it diving to Davy Jones's locker, 'Jonah' began in *The Beano* on 15 March 1958; many of the scripts were written by Walter Fearne, an experi-

A colour plate from a painting by Ken Reid and featured in '*Fudge's Trip to the Moon*' (London University Press: 1947). The elf is in the background peeping out from behind a boulder; centre-stage is an 'extraordinary creature' typical of many of Reid's creations in 'Fudge'. This one is a good example of his talent for the 'comic grotesque'.

JONAH
IN
AND WE MEAN 'IM'
"DOPY MICK" PART ONE
MOBY DICK, THAT FABULOUS WHITE WHALE OF A BYGONE ERA, IS BUT A LEGEND TODAY! BUT, STILL RANGING THE ANTARCTIC WASTES, IS HIS DIRECT DESCENDANT, DOPY MICK.
PHOO!
GONE, TOO, IS THAT EMBITTERED HUNTER OF MOBY DICK, CAP'N AHAB OF THE "PEQUOD"! BUT STILL VERY MUCH ALIVE AND KICKING IS HIS GREAT, GREAT NEPHEW, CAP'N MALCOLM McBLUBBER OF THE WHALING SHIP "PEAPOD"—AND SO THE FEUD CONTINUES!
GRR! AH'LL HUNT YE DOON YET, DOPY MICK! SNARL!
LOOK WHIT YON BLUBBER-BOUND FIEND DID TAE ME ON MA LAST TRIP! HE SWALLOWED MA PEG-LEG WHEN IT ROLLED OVER-BOARD—
—AN' IT COST ME 5/- SECOND-HAND!
BUT AH'LL GET MY REVENGE. AYE—SNARL!—AH'LL PUT A HARPOON IN YON OVERFED LUMP O' BLUBBER THIS VERRA DAY—
—OR BUST!
EEK!
SWISH-H!
BAM!
ER-MORNIN', CAP'N—
BLUBBER
—I—ER—HOPPED ABOARD AT SOUTH GEORGIA WHILE YOU WERE RE-FUELLIN'! GULP! I THOUGHT YOU MIGHT BE GLAD OF AN EXTRA BLUBBER-BASHER! HEH-HEH-HEH!
AGH-H-H! HELP! S.O.S! MAYDAY! IT'S 'IM! WE'RE AS GOOD AS SUNK! ALL HANDS ON DECK!
ALL HANDS CHARGE UP ON DECK, DETERMINED TO SAVE THEIR SHIP—AND THEY DO....
HUP!
YOU ROTTEN, IGNORANT SWABS!
AARGH!
BLOOP!
GLUG! GULP! GURGLE!
THEN, AFTER FOUR HOURS OF GLUGGING, GULPING AND GURGLING IN THE COLD BRINY—
GOODY! MY LUCK'S IN! A LITTLE SNOW-COVERED ISLAND! I CAN BUILD AN IGLOO ON IT AN' WAIT THERE TILL ANOTHER SHIP SHOWS UP!
BUT, JUST AS JONAH IS APPROACHING THE LITTLE, SNOW-COVERED "ISLAND"—IT YAWNS!
AR-R-H-H-H!
ERK!
WHAT'S HAPPENING?
HELP! S.O.S!
RUMBLE!
GURGLE!
BLIMEY! WHERE AM I? GLUB!
SPLAT!
I'M IN A DARK, PINK, GURGLING CAVERN! AN' THE ONLY PIECE OF FURNITURE IS AN OLD PEG-LEG!
BOILK!
A PEG-LEG! ERK! CAP'N McBLUBBER'S PEG-LEG! I-I'M IN DOPY MICK'S TUM!
BLEWP!
I'VE BEEN SWALLOWED BY A WHALE!
HELP! LEMME OUT-A HERE! GASP!
THUD! THUD! SQUELCH!
BLUR-RP!
FOR PETE'S SAKE, SNEEZE OR SOMETHING!
NOW JONAH KNOWS HOW HIS NAME-SAKE FELT! —AND OUR SEA-GOON ISN'T JUST IN THE WHALE'S TUM FOR THREE DAYS AND THREE NIGHTS —HE'S STUCK HERE RIGHT THROUGH TO PART TWO, NEXT WEEK! DON'T MISS IT!

enced sub-editor who later became an editor. Reid and Fearne worked in tandem to produce what was to become a classic strip: Fearne's funny scripts made provision for about 12 pictures; Reid would then seize on particular incidents and use them to create additional scenes. Consequently, a page would contain an unusually high number of panels, up to 36 pictures in many cases. The result was some of the most hilarious, best-drawn comic pages of the 1950s and 1960s. Within weeks of its debut, 'Jonah' was the most popular feature in *The Beano*.

Ken Reid drew 'Jonah' continuously for the next few years, both for the weekly comic and *The Beano Book*, its annual. The publisher occasionally forwarded some of the voluminous fan mail 'Jonah' generated. One letter revealed, not surprisingly, that Jonah was popular with the Royal Navy: the ship's crew of HMS *Victorious* wrote and requested a drawing of Jonah for their mess; Reid complied with a life-size black and white original for them to hang on their bulkhead.

Illness interfered with his career

'The Nervs' were the nightmarish inhabitants of the body of an obese schoolboy. The idea was outlandish to begin with, but in Reid's hands it bordered on the insane. The sets overleaf were published in *Smash!* on 9 November 1968.

© Fleetway Publications, London, 1989.

Opposite
'Jonah' was the finest of all Ken Reid's work. The script would probably have been written by Walter Fearne, with considerable embellishment by Reid. The page shown here is part of one of several classic 'Jonah' serials published in the *Beano* in the late Fifties and early Sixties. Each picture is a comic masterpiece, from Captain Ahab's reaction to his discovery of Jonah in the barrel, through to the last picture with the goon hammering his fists against the stomach lining of the whale.

© D.C. Thomson & Co. Ltd.

The NERVS
HOW'S THAT, FOLKS! A WHOLE TEN BOB TO SPEND ON FIREWORKS!
TUM DEPT.
BAH! WHY SHOULD THAT FAT TWERP HAVE ALL THE FUN?
IT'S TIME US NERVS HAD A BIT OF HILARITY!
BUT ONE OF FATTY'S TUM NERVS DOESN'T SHARE HIS ENTHUSIASM.
SO SAYING, "BOUNCER" BOYNGS TO THE BRAIN DEPT.—
THOUGHT MACHINE
GOODIE! THE BRAIN NERVS HAVE GONE FOR A CUPPA, LEAVING OLD "DOZEY" IN CHARGE OF THE THOUGHT-MACHINE!
CONVEYOR TUBE
POST MESSAGE
PULL TO FLASH IT TO FATTY'S BONCE
I'LL SEND FATTY A MESSAGE THAT'LL CHANGE HIS INTENTIONS. THE BIG NIT WON'T BE ABLE TO RESIST THE THOUGHT OF SWEETS.
DON'T WASTE YOUR LOLLY ON FIRE-WORKS, FATTY! THINK OF THE OODLES OF SHERBERT FIZZ YOU COULD BUY.
AND SO—
PUSH
PULL
NOW TO ZIP IT TO FATTY'S BRAIN-BOX BY PULLING THIS HANDLE.
CLICK
THE NEXT SECOND, FATTY GETS THE MESSAGE.—
CLICK
DON'T—WASTE—YOUR—LOLLY—ON—FIREWORKS—FATTY! THINK—OF—THE—OODLES—OF—SHERBERT—FIZZ—YOU—COULD—BUY!
COR!! I'VE JUST HAD A SCRUMPTIOUS IDEA!
AND, AFTER A BLIND, UNREASONING STUMBLE TO THE NEAREST SWEET AND SHERBERT SHOP—
FIZZ-Z-Z
FIZZ-Z-Z
AH-H! WHO WANTS FIREWORKS, ANYWAY?
SLUR-RP
FIZZ
SHERBERT EXTRA FIZZY
THE ANSWER TO THAT FIZZ-BEFUDDLED QUESTION LIES IN THE TUM DEPT. FOLKS—
QUICK, CHAPS! BRING THOSE UNDIGESTED LENGTHS OF MACARONI HE SLURPED FOR LUNCH. WE'LL FILL 'EM WITH FIZZ!
FOOD TUBE
WE DO!!— AND HERE COMES THE FIZZ TO MAKE SOME!
YA-HOO!
FIZZ
HIC! BURP!
SO, FIFTY YARDS OF MACARONI LATER—
WATCH OUT, LADS! WE'RE LETTING "WONEYE'S" HOME-MADE RIP-RAP OFF!
FIZZ-Z-Z
HEE-HEE! GUESS WHO!
FIZZ-Z-Z-Z-Z
FIZZ
NIT!
FIZZ
PHOO
1d FOR THE GUY
LUVLY!
UN-GNASHED MACARONI.- FOR MECHANICAL CHOMPING.
HALF-WAY THROUGH THE ABDOMINAL-"FIREWORKS"—
DOH-H!! ERK!
MUM! HELP! I'VE JUST HAD EIGHTEEN SHERBERTS AN' SOMETHIN' FUNNY'S HAPPENIN' TO ME!
HIC!
BANG
BLOYLK
HUH! I KNOW WHAT YOU NEED, M'LAD!
WHOOPH -ZIZZ-Z
FIZZ
RUMBLE

several times and at one stage he was unable to work for almost a year. But whenever possible he was prepared to take on additional comic pages. One of these was 'Ali Ha-Ha and the Forty Thieves' (1960); others were 'Big Head and Thick Head' and 'Jinx' (both c. 1963) as well as his work for *The Beano* annual. At this time Reid was earning £18 for each page he submitted, excellent remuneration 30 years ago. But in 1964 he was contacted by the London-based Odhams Press who told him they were starting a new comic, *Wham!* Odhams offered Reid £30 per page, an offer he felt he couldn't refuse, and as a result he soon left D. C. Thomson.

When Alf Wallace, the managing editor at Odhams Press, and Albert Cosser, editor of *Wham!*, met Ken Reid to discuss ideas, Reid mentioned his penchant for comic horror, and

There was little editorial control at Odhams Press and, left to his own devices, Reid was able to give full expression to his zany humour. In this glorious two-pager for *Smash!*, 12 March 1966, his northern origins give that humour an added dimension. Witness 'The Buoyant Queen' rigged out Heath Robinson fashion as a Kipper-Catcher, while, in the last picture, about to steam over the horizon is another ship 'heading for Honolulu with a cargo of black treacle'. Reid's stock-in-trade was the bizarre turn of events. In this example he has excelled himself as the Kipper-Catcher begins to take to the air. © Fleetway Publications, London, 1989.

SEAS
BUOYANT QUEEN
200 JERKS LATER...
I'M OUT, BERT!
CRIKEY! I MUST HAVE BEEN STUCK FOR HOURS! IT'S GORN DARK AND I CAN'T SEE A THING!
THROB!
MOAN! SPLASH! GROAN! SPLOSH!
BERT! WHERE ARE YOU? IT'S PITCH BLACK OUT HERE! I CAN'T SEE YOU, MATE!
GROPE
SPLOOSH! GROAN! SPLOSH! CROAK!
SPLUTCH!
SLIPPERY 'SEA-SQUOYLP.'
TRY TO GROAN LOUDER - SO'S I CAN FOLLOW THE SOUND - !! ERK!
ZIP
SKID!
ENOCH GRABS THE RIM OF THE WHIRLING 'HERRING-CURER'!
WHIR-R-R-
GRAB!
?????
-AND, 500 REVOLUTIONS LATER...
AGH-H! TURN-IT-OFF! (GASP! WHEEZE!) I'M BEIN' KIPPERED!
WHIZZ-Z-
STOP PLAYIN' MERRY-GO-ROUNDS AND HELP ME! HELP!
SPLOSH! SPLASH! SPLOOSH!
-I'M GOING ROUND AN' ROUND- IN AND OUT OF THE FLIPPIN' PACIFIC- WITH A WALKIN' JELLYFISH ON ME LAP! HELP!!
AFTER 25,000 REVOLUTIONS, ENOCH HAS BEEN WHIZZED FLAT - LIKE A HELICOPTER BLADE!
HELP! THE ENGINE'S GOIN' SO FAST WE'RE TAKING OFF!
HUM-M-M-
WHEE-E-E
MEANWHILE, ON THE HORIZON, A CAREFREE CAPTAIN IS CONFIDENT THAT HE'S HEADING FOR HONOLULU, WITH A CARGO OF BLACK TREACLE. JOIN THIS POOR WRETCH NEXT WEEK, SHIPMATES - BUT WEAR YOUR LIFE-JACKETS!
Ken Reid.

Faceache made his first appearance on 8 May 1971, in *Jet*. When this title was discontinued he moved to *Buster*, billed as 'The Boy With A Hundred Faces' (it later became a thousand!). To some, he was a lad who could merely change shape, but Reid once gave a more detailed explanation: 'I worked in the "Scrunge", an effect which could change his whole atomic structure . . . contracting and expanding his molecules in order that he (could) become almost anything.' Throughout the Seventies Ken Reid wrote and drew Faceache every week and was responsible for some of the most innovative comic art of the time.
© Fleetway Publications, London, 1989.

Wallace promptly suggested a parody of Frankenstein entitled 'Frankie Stein'. The idea delighted Reid and he enthusiastically set about designing the character and then writing and drawing the feature each week for *Wham!* Cosser and Wallace gave Reid a completely free hand, which allowed him to indulge in wild fantasy and some outrageous scripting. As a result, 'Frankie Stein' was hugely popular. This popularity was extended to later years when it passed into the hands of another artist, Bob Nixon; and the character still appears today, 25 years on.

Another comic character drawn and written by Reid for *Wham!* was 'Jasper the Grasper'. Jasper was an innovation: he was a rich miser, living in Victorian England. This was a different and highly original setting for a comic character, as was typical of Reid. This feature was also a hit, appearing in other titles long after the comic's demise. *Wham!* was discontinued on 13 January 1968, a short run but judged a 'qualified success' by the publishers (since the 1960s there have been several new titles that haven't lasted six months). But long before that, on 5 February 1965, *Wham!* was provided with a companion comic called *Smash!*

For *Smash!* Reid was asked to emulate his earlier success with 'Jonah' by contributing a two-pager entitled 'Queen of the Seas'. This was the tale of an old steamship operated by two sailors each endowed with characteristic Ken Reid lunacy. Although not as hilarious as 'Jonah', it was extremely funny and Reid's art was superb. He also took over another two-page feature entitled 'The Nervs'. The setting of this wonderfully drawn comic strip was the human body, and the characters were the micro-organ-

isms which lived within it. At the time it was one of the most original features to appear in a weekly comic, and today remains one of the most memorable.

When *Wham!* was discontinued, *Smash!* continued its run until Odhams Press was acquired by the International Publishing Corporation (IPC) in 1969. Shortly afterwards *Smash!* was merged with IPC's own *Valiant* and Reid found himself temporarily unemployed. He decided to take a long holiday and purchased a canal boat. Sadly, but to the considerable amusement of his friends, the boat sank while he was ashore. It seemed for a while that Jonah had returned to haunt him. . . .

IPC had no wish to leave Ken Reid without work for long. At the end of 1969 he was asked to contribute to *Scorcher*, a weekly with football as its theme. For this he drew several unexceptional pages, none of which was worthy of note. But in 1971 he began to draw 'Faceache' for a new comic, *Jet*. Initially, Faceache was a young lad who could pull horrendous faces; but it became far more than that as Reid gradually extended his powers by use of what he called a 'Scrunge'. The Scrunge was an effect which, Reid said, could alter Faceache's atomic structure, contracting and expanding his molecules so that he could become almost anything. Faceache was to run for years, al-

An excerpt from a later episode of Faceache at Belmont School; probably not written by Reid, it nevertheless gave him the opportunity to draw the effects of three different Scrunges. This page features Faceache's common adversary, Mr Snipe, who possessed the most remarkable cranium. Note panel 2 for a detailed study.
© Fleetway Publications, London, 1989.

though not in *Jet*, which ended its short run with a record 21 issues.

When *Jet* was abruptly discontinued, 'Faceache' was transferred to the successful weekly title, *Buster*, which began in 1969 and is still running. As well as drawing 'Faceache', Reid wrote the scripts throughout most of the 1970s. He made the comic character unique in possessing a strong northern accent, although this was later phased out in favour of standard non-regional speech. Later, Faceache's Scrunge became more outlandish and horrific, much to the delight of readers and sending Reid's work to the top of the list of readers' favourites.

Yet another excuse for Reid to indulge in comic horror was 'Martha's Monster Makeup' (*Monster Fun*: 1975). One dab of this potent mixture (which never ran out!) turned whatever it touched into something monstrous. The variety of horrors that flowed from Reid's pen seemed infinite.
© Fleetway Publications, London, 1989.

Reid's quirky sense of humour combined once again with the macabre in the 1970s in a feature that he suggested to IPC: his idea was for the central character to be suicidal, attempting each week to kill himself, only to be thwarted somehow in the last picture. The then editor said later, 'It was hilarious; classic Ken Reid, but we simply couldn't publish it in a children's comic at the time, considering the subject matter. It was ahead of its time, but it had the office in stitches!' As the editor said: classic Ken Reid. . . .

Drawing on Ken Reid's abilities to create magnificently funny monsters, IPC's editors created a new series specifically for him. This was 'Creepy Creations' which appeared on the back page of a new comic entitled *Shiver & Shake* (1973). 'Creepy Creations' was a series of nearly page-size pen and ink drawings (printed in colour) of monsters such as 'The Horrible Estate Eater from Eton' (it

Putting to good use Ken Reid's zany humour and his talent for the creation of comic horrors, Bob Paynter, the editor of two Seventies' comics, *Whoopee*! and *Shiver & Shake*, commissioned him to draw three different series of weird gag pictures. Those shown here combine puns with black comedy in drawings that would have been well-suited to *Mad* magazine!
© Fleetway Publications, London, 1989.

The drawings shown here are reproduced from originals several times the size. On the left is 'The London Scareport'; on the right, 'The Fright Cliffs of Dover'. Reid's monsters here are horrifically real. He never skimped on detail and went to enormous lengths to achieve the effect he required.
© Fleetway Publications, London, 1989.

actually devoured housing estates!), 'The Crab-Nosed Clodhopper from Cleethorpes' and many others. The majority were suggested by readers and the concept was successful enough for Reid to be asked to do two other series: 'Wanted Posters' and 'World Wide Weirdies', both appearing in another new weekly, *Whoopee*!, which began publication in 1974.

The horror craze peaked when, in 1975, IPC launched a weekly which consisted of nothing but comic strips based on monsters. This was named, appropriately enough, *Monster Fun*. Ken Reid's contribution was 'Martha's Monster Makeup', a one-pager about a young girl who, when she applied her special make-up, would be turned into something monstrous. After this he drew 'Tom Horror's World', a skit on the television programme, 'Tomorrow's World', which appeared in *Wow!* until that comic was amalgamated with *Whoopee!* in 1983.

Ken Reid died on 2 February 1987. He was still drawing 'Faceache', although he had not written it for some years, scripts being supplied by various freelance writers (one of whom is the author of this book), which never matched his own high standard. He was sadly missed. His art and peculiar brand of humour were unique, not only in this country but anywhere in the world. His fans hailed from many countries and he would always gladly reply to their letters if they took the trouble to write. A genuinely modest man, he would have been astonished that his death was reported in large obituaries in leading newspapers such as *The Times* and the *Daily Telegraph*. Ken Reid's stories and drawings were as British as fish and chips or Yorkshire pudding; he managed beautifully the difficult task of combining his superior comic art with a macabre humour which in the world of comics will be impossible to replace.

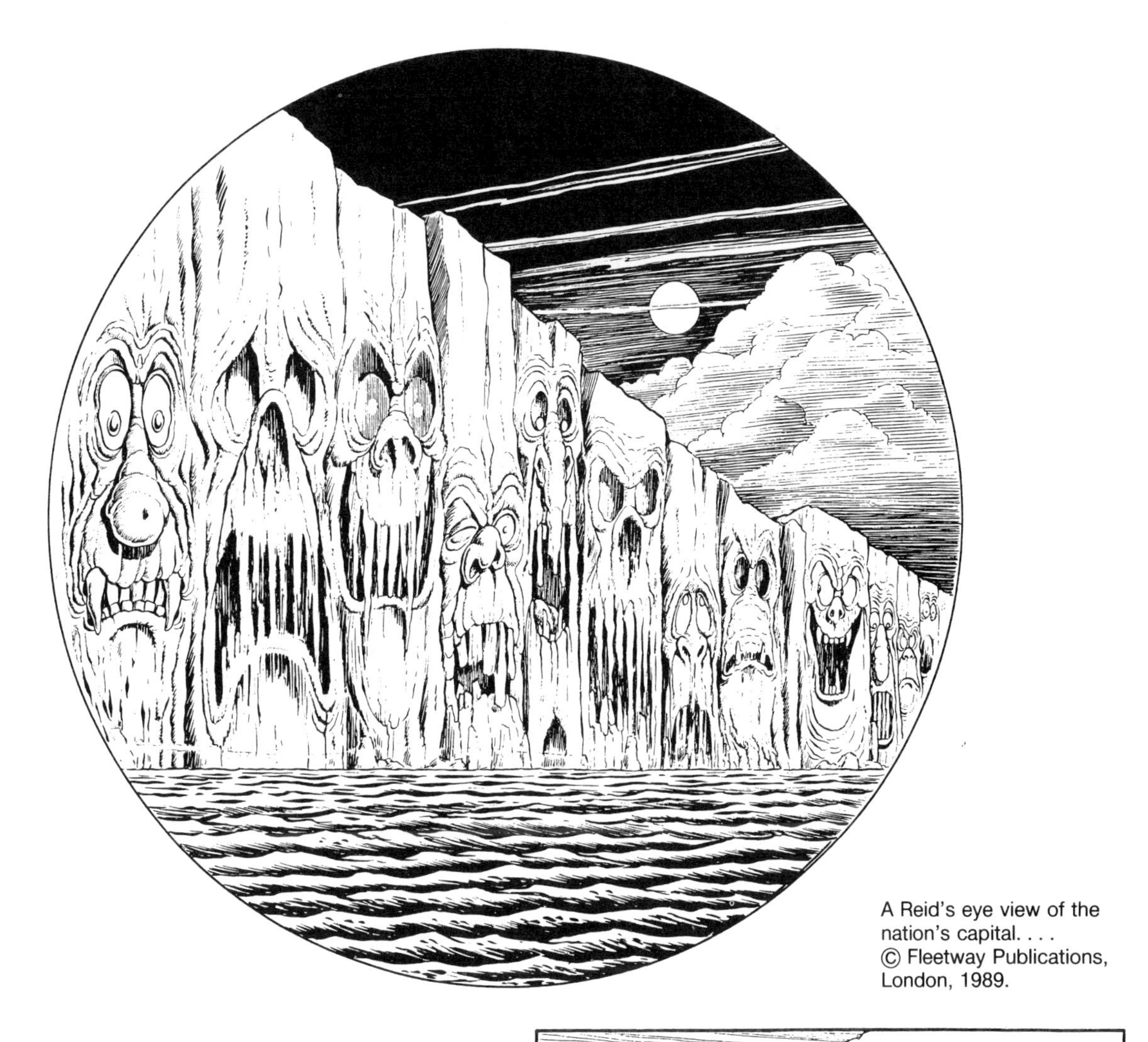

A Reid's eye view of the nation's capital. . . .
© Fleetway Publications, London, 1989.

Further Reading

A Very Funny Business Leo Baxendale
British Comic World (Issues 1–5) Alan & David Coates
Who's Who of Boys Writers & Illustrators Brian Doyle
Encyclopedia of Comic Characters Denis Gifford
The International Book of Comics Denis Gifford
The Wonderful World of Film Fun Graham King & Ron Saxby
Old Boys Books: A Complete Catalogue W.O.G. Lofts & D.J. Adley
Catalogue of Boys and Girls Annuals W. O. G. Lofts & D. J. Adley
The Penguin Book of Comics George Perry & Alan Aldridge
Fudge in Bubbleville Ken Reid/Savoy Books
Fudge and The Dragon Ken Reid/Savoy Books
Boys Will Be Boys E. S. Turner
The Dandy Monster Index (Vols 1 + 2) Ray Moore

Index